THE MESSIAH
CONQUERS
THE WHITE HOUSE

Uncover the Sacred Weapons of the First
African American President
of the United States

The Greatest Revelation of the Twenty-First Century

I myself will prepare your way, leveling mountains and hills. I will break
down bronze gates and smash their iron bars. I will give you treasures
from dark, secret places; then you will know that I am the Lord, and that
the God of Israel has called you by name.

(Isaiah 45:2–3)

Aying Godman
Christian Mystic, Numerologist, and Biblical Scholar
Lay Catholic Charismatic Minister

iUniverse LLC
Bloomington

The Messiah Conquers the White House
Uncover the Sacred Weapons of the First African American
President of the United States

Scriptures quoted from the Good News Bible published by The United Bible Societies © American Bible Society, 1966, 1971, 1976, and 1992.[1]

iUniverse books may be ordered through booksellers or by contacting:

iUniverse LLC
1663 Liberty Drive
Bloomington, IN 47403
www.iuniverse.com
1-800-Authors (1-800-288-4677)

ISBN: 978-1-4917-0145-4 (sc)
ISBN: 978-1-4917-0146-1 (e)

Library of Congress Control Number: 2013917160

Printed in the United States of America.

iUniverse rev. date: 10/19/2013

---

1.   This acknowledgment is in accordance with the provisions of the Quotation Rights for the *Good News Bible* as stated on page vii of the *Good News Bible* and, therefore, satisfies the requirements for the use of quotations from this Bible in *The Messiah Conquers the White House.*

In

Loving Memory

Of

Glory Aying

.

CONTENTS

Symbols

Sun
Zero
Cross
Dot and Circle
Straight Line Linking Two Points
Equilateral Triangle
Perfect Square
Pentagram
Perfect Square in Perfect Square
Positive and Negative Signs in Circle
Frog
Gnat
Fly
Head of Bull and Cross
Boils
Hailstones
Locust
Black Sphere
Human Head and Cross
Turning Wheel
Orb

FOREWORD

THE Messiah² Conquers the White House is written for the general public and, especially, for readers interested in spirituality, philosophy, numerology, the mysteries, and divine manifestations.

The purpose of this book is to uncover the hidden knowledge of the fulfillment of the holy scriptures in Barack Obama, the first African American president of the United States. It explains the part played by numbers, virtues, and divine forces in the accession of Barack Obama to power and in his victories in the presidency.

This revelation is expected to show the mighty power of God at work in our time. Thus, you will understand and appreciate, in their true value, the various events happening in America and in the rest of the world under the administration and diplomacy of President Barack Obama. The wonderful story of Barack Obama should also serve as an inspiration to all those who desire to make things happen—that through faith and self-awareness they can turn their misfortunes into lifetime fortunes.

What is fascinating about this book is the unique combination of scripture, biography, politics, and numerology³ to support the divine ordination⁴ of Barack Obama and his messianic mission to the White House.

Aying Godman

2. The **Messiah** is Jesus Christ the Son of God and Savior of the world. The word *Messiah*, which means "anointed one," is used figuratively as the title of Barack Obama, who is "chosen" by God to save America and the rest of the world from injustice, inequality, and instability.

3. **Numerology** is the scientific and mystical study of numbers and number symbolism to determine the invisible spiritual forces that influence the lives and activities of people.

4. **Ordination** is the state of being chosen in advance and empowered by God to fulfill a given mission.

PREFACE

THE idea of writing *The Messiah Conquers the White House* was sparked off by the awe-inspiring victory of Barack Obama in the 2008 presidential election to become the first African American president of the United States. The event prompted me to look for the forces that propelled him to power, and in my research I was graciously led to the arsenal of the sacred weapons with which the "anointed" one fights and wins in battles.

My investigation began with the courageous declared intention of then Senator Barack Obama in 2006 to run for the White House, despite his relative political inexperience and "bad" black color, in a multiracial United States dominated by whites. His rhetoric was outstanding and his charm irresistible. He rapidly became a crowd puller, winning acclamation in the Democratic Party conventions. And then he received his party's nomination for the powerful and prestigious presidency of the United States, which he won with ease.

With a keen interest and mystical[5a] insight, I studied the biography of Barack Obama, identifying his vital[5b] numbers, virtues, and biblical correspondence. By correlating his life with the scriptures and analyzing the symbolism of his numbers, I found both his correspondence with the Lord Jesus Christ and his holy weapons of war.

On the basis of scriptures and numerology, I established the thesis of the unbeatable power of Barack Obama and his messianic mission to the White House and prophesied that he would receive a second mandate to rule the United States of America. The unfolding of events between the first inauguration of President Barack Obama on January 20, 2009, and his reelection on November 6, 2012, gave full credibility to the claim I now put forward in *The Messiah Conquers the White House*. I give praise and glory to Jesus Christ our Lord for his superabundant grace to me.

Aying Godman
June 23, 2013

5a. Connected with **mysticism**—the search for truth through prayer and meditation.

5b. The **vital numbers** of an individual are those numbers that are both recurrent and significant to that person and are, therefore, active in the events that occur in his or her life.

Acknowledgments

I sincerely thank all those who gave me moral, material, and financial help during the writing and production of this book.

My profound gratitude goes to Thekla Indah, Ivo Ngang, Adeline Mbanwi, Raphael Mbanwi, Olga Njomeni, Bernard Tatah, and Glory Aying. I wish all of them God's blessings, prosperity, and abundant life.

Aying Godman

INTRODUCTION

THE Messiah Conquers the White House combines scripture, biography, politics, philosophy, and numerology to uncover a mysterious and startling correspondence between the Nativity, infancy, revelation, crucifixion, resurrection, and ascension of Jesus Christ into heaven and the conception, birth, childhood, revelation, and accession of Barack Obama to the White House. It presents the first-ever African American president of the United States as a messiah anointed by God to bring freedom, equality, justice, and peace to America and the whole world. *The Messiah Conquers the White House* examines the sacred weapons of Barack Obama, which enabled him to win the US presidency twice, and with which he fights and wins political, economic, social, diplomatic, and military battles from the White House. The sacred weapons of Barack Obama are found in the scriptures fulfilling in him, and in the numbers and virtues that characterize his life.

The Power of the Scriptures

The holy scriptures, as the living and eternal Word of God (Hebrews 4:12; Matthew 5:17–18), are the vehicles of God's power and divine manifestations (Isaiah 55:10–11). In conformity with the plan of God (Isaiah 48:3–8), they are fulfilled at all times in people and in events that affect the world and constantly shape the history of humanity.

At different times God chooses different people and uses them to bring about the fulfillment of his Word. These choices depend solely on the will and grace of God, and so no one can boast of his or her merits (Ephesians 2:6–9). Such anointed people have included the prophet Moses (Exodus 3), King David (Samuel 16:1–13), and Emperor Cyrus (Isaiah 45:1–13; 48:12–16). The choice of Barack Obama today as a messiah in the United States is another fulfillment of the scriptures in Micah 5:2, 4–5: "The Lord says, 'Bethlehem Ephrathah, you are one of the smallest towns in Judah, but out of you I will bring a ruler for Israel, whose family line goes back to ancient times.' When he comes, he will rule his people with the strength that comes from the Lord and with the majesty of the Lord God himself. His people will live in safety because people all over the earth will acknowledge his greatness, and he will bring peace."

Besides, *The Messiah Conquers the White House* examines two biblical mysteries that correspond perfectly to Barack Obama and which stand out to prove his divine ordination as president of the United States of America and messiah of the twenty-first century. These are the mysteries of the Nativity in Bethlehem and the death of John the Baptist before the self-revelation of the Master and Lord Jesus Christ.

The Power of Numbers

Every number (inclusive from zero to nine) is a sign that represents a specific idea, force, or principle. Numbers are not dead signs, but rather are abbreviated expressions of active principles and divine forces whose texts are written in the very mind of God. The power of numbers is real and effective, and numbers exert a great influence on human beings, nature, and life.

Numerology is the scientific and mystical study of numbers and number symbolism to determine the invisible spiritual forces that influence the lives and activities of people. This system uses the method of numerical reduction[6] to bring every number down to one digit in order to determine its symbolism and examine its influence on the person to whom it relates. This book identifies and examines six vital numbers of Barack Obama (one, two, three, four, five, and eight), whose powers influence his life and activities from the spiritual plane.

The Power of Virtues

The virtues that every person has are expressions of divine perfection because God created human beings in his own image and likeness (Genesis 1:26–27). Therefore, the specific qualities of people are the vehicles of divine grace and power for their own fulfillment. Virtues are either inborn or cultivated through the grace of God (Matthew 7:7–8). Thus, in accordance with his or her virtues, everyone has the capacity to overcome obstacles in order to break through in life.

The ten great virtues of Barack Obama are faith, courage, excellence, love, uniqueness, charm, oratory, diligence, serenity, and hope. They represent the ten great plagues[7] (Exodus 7–12) that God unleashed against the king of Egypt to free the Israelites after 430 years of slavery (Exodus 2:40–41).

An Arsenal of Weapons

Evidently, the journey of Barack Obama from "nothingness" to the helm of power passed through stages of education, training, and experimentation. These enabled him to bring out the powers of his vital numbers and inborn virtues. His spectacular breakthrough resulted from a combination of spiritual and material forces working under the mighty power of God. A close study of the scriptures, and the numbers and virtues of Barack Obama, uncovers the mysteries[8] of his being. It throws extra light on his powers, his winning spirit, and the significance of his accession to the White House.

The two biblical mysteries relating to Barack Obama, his six vital numbers, and his ten powerful virtues constitute the mighty arsenal of his holy weapons. This book explains how he used these invisible weapons to conquer the White House, how they impact on the Obama America, and how they would shape the post-Obama world.

The Cornerstone

Definitely, *The Messiah Conquers the White House* states and proves that Barack Obama is not an ordinary human being, although he is also not Jesus Christ of Nazareth, and that his election in 2008 and reelection in 2012 as the forty-fourth president of the United States were ordained by God and mysteriously calculated to happen in time and space. The purpose, it holds, is to form a better world order in the twenty-first century by building a foundation of freedom, equality, justice, and peace on the cornerstone of Barack Obama in the White House. "For the scripture says: 'I chose a valuable stone, which I am placing as the corner stone in Zion; and whoever believes in him will never be disappointed.' This stone is of great value for you that believe; but for those who do not believe: 'The stone which the builders rejected as worthless turned out to be the most important of all.' And another scripture says: 'This is the stone that will make people stumble, the rock that will make them fall.' They stumbled because they did not believe in the word; such was God's will for them. But you are the chosen race, the King's priests, the holy nation, God's own people, chosen to proclaim the wonderful acts of God, who called you out of darkness into his own marvelous light" (1 Peter 2:6–9).

The prologue will give us a snapshot of the historic election of Barack Obama as the first-ever African American president of the United States.

---

6. **Numerical reduction** is the process of adding the digits of a number repeatedly to arrive at a single digit.
7. A **plague** is a large number of insects, animals, or some other thing that comes into a place and causes great damage.
8. **Mysteries** are secret knowledge of somebody or something accessible only by divine revelation or spiritual insight.

Artwork 1 of 21: Sun. This is the symbol of
excellence, brilliance, and glory.

The Glory of God

The Word became a human being and, full of grace and truth, lived among us. We saw his glory, the glory which he received as the Father's only Son.

(John 1:14)

ON November 4, 2008, a certain Barack Hussein Obama, Democratic US senator from Illinois, was elected to the White House as the forty-fourth president of the United States of America. The event stormed America and the whole world with wonder and surprise. For, although he had led in the opinion polls ahead of his Republican rival, Senator John McCain, no one really believed that it was time for an African American to rule the United States.

That day was marked by popular and spontaneous celebrations throughout the United States and many other countries. President-Elect Barack Obama received instant messages of congratulations from numerous world leaders. They included leaders of countries that are traditionally opposed to the United States: President Mahmoud Ahmadinejad of

Iran, President Mahmoud Abbas of the Palestinian National Authority, and the leader of Hamas—Khaled Meshaal. In fact, on that historic occasion the Secretary-General of the Arab League, Amr Moussa, said, "The world has a new leader in Barack Obama," and "Barack Obama could bring about a sea of change in the Middle East." In addition to that, some countries like Kenya, the birthplace of Mr. Obama's father, declared a public holiday to celebrate the event. Besides, many babies born on the night of November 4 through November 5, 2008, were given the first names of Barack, Obama, or Michelle. Since then, many Baracks, Obamas, and Michelles have been born across the world to those who admire and support the icon and his wife.

Moreover, since the election of Barack Obama as president of the United States, his name has become not only a household word but also a famous brand name. Articles ranging from shoes to clothing and from writing materials to traveling bags now carry the image and name of Barack Obama. Also, his name is the chorus of many hit songs from Africa and around the world. The spirit of Obamamania[9] has grown into a worldwide force as Barack Obama becomes the most spectacular phenomenon[10] of the twenty-first century.

If the foregoing discussion proves that the election of Barack Obama to the White House was not an ordinary event, there are even more signs to show that it was not just a stroke of good fortune. In fact, when Barack Obama was born on August 4, 1961, and until his election on November 4, 2008, it was still a stigma to be black in America. How, then, did he transform his handicap into an advantage, making a swift and spectacular rise to the most powerful and prestigious presidency in the world? Certainly, he worked hard to unfold the virtues of his being, and this pushed him to the forefront of politics as a competent and dependable leader, especially in times of unprecedented financial crisis and diplomatic hostility.

However, the glorious victories of Barack Obama cannot be fully justified by objective and human factors alone. There is very strong evidence that spiritual forces played a fundamental role in his rise to power. The nature and magnitude of these forces can be perceived only from a mystical perspective, and understanding them is necessary to fully unravel the mystery[11] of Barack Obama. In fact, the unveiling of this mystery is essential to understanding the mission assigned to him by God. Everything that happens in this world happens at the time that God chooses (Ecclesiastes 3:1), and the mystery of Barack Obama is as deep as the issues that challenge him in the White House.

On January 20, 2009, Barack Obama was inaugurated for the first time as the president of the United States. The inauguration took place in the presence of two million people gathered in Washington, DC, from all over the world. On November 6, 2012, he faced former Massachusetts Republican Governor Mitt Romney in a fierce battle for reelection. Barack Obama, armed with his most holy weapons, was again unbeatable. He won, in spite of his poor score for the performance of the US economy, receiving 332 out of the 538 electoral votes, and over sixty-five million popular votes. He also won twenty-six states and the District of Columbia.

The second presidential inauguration of Barack Obama took place on Monday, January 21, 2013, on Capitol Hill. But before then, on January 1, 2013, he prevented the much-dreaded "fiscal cliff" by successfully pushing the US Senate and House of Representatives to pass his bill on tax increases for the top 2 percent of richest Americans. There, he won another battle against the Republicans, who had been opposed to such a tax increase, and fulfilled one of his key 2012 campaign promises. Thus began the second round of victories for Barack Obama in the White House—and the greatest is yet to come. The question, then, is, what are the sacred weapons of Barack Obama, and how does he win? The answers to these questions are the subject of the discussion in this book.

In chapter 1, we will discuss the signs that show that Barack Obama, like Jesus Christ, was born in the manger.

9. **Mania** is an extremely strong desire, enthusiasm, or love for something shared by many people at the same time. Hence, Obamamania is the shared and powerful spirit of love and admiration for Barack Obama.

10. A **phenomenon** is a person who is very successful and impressive.

11. A **mystery** is something that is difficult to understand or explain, or a person who is strange and interesting because very little or nothing is known about him or her.

Artwork 2 of 21: Zero. This is the symbol of
nothingness, poverty, and humility.

CHAPTER ONE

The Signs of the Manger

The Lord says, "Bethlehem Ephrathah, you
are one of the smallest towns in Judah, but
out of you I will bring a ruler for Israel, whose
family line goes back to ancient times."

(Micah 5:2)

THE birth of Barack Hussein Obama Jr., son of Barack
Hussein Obama and Stanley Ann Dunham, in the Pacific
archipelago of Hawaii was not an accident. This, together
with his stay in Indonesia, his upbringing in Hawaii, and his
eventual settlement in the city of Chicago, has a mysterious
relationship with the greatest event in the history of mankind—
the Nativity of Jesus Christ in Bethlehem. They marked the
coming of a messiah in the hubs of humility and diversity.
There was the man Barack Obama, being ordained by his
blood, birth, and upbringing to save the United States and
the rest of the world from the evils of the twenty-first century:
oppression, inequality, injustice, and war.

The Incarnation

The coming of Barack Obama into the world was, therefore, a reenactment of the Nativity—although Barack Obama is not Jesus Christ and is in no way equal to him. Barack Obama is a man who was born to be a god, but Jesus Christ is God who was born to be a man. This is affirmed by the scriptures in John 1:14: "The Word became a human being and, full of grace and truth, lived among us. We saw his glory, the glory which he received as the Father's only Son." And in Philippians 2:6–7, it is written, "He [Jesus Christ] always had the nature of God, but he did not think that by force he should try to remain equal with God. Instead of this, of his own free will he gave up all he had, and took the nature of a servant. He became like a human being and appeared in human likeness." In fact, Jesus of Nazareth had a universal spiritual and human mission that was unlimited in time and scope, whereas Barack Obama has a universal political and social mission that is limited in scope and time.

We will establish the correspondences between Barack Obama and Jesus Christ by examining the circumstances of their births and their lives. Thus we will unravel the mystery of the election of Barack Obama as the first African American president of the United States of America.

Hawaii and Bethlehem

It is written in Luke 2:1–7:

> At that time the Emperor Augustus ordered a census to be taken throughout the Roman Empire. When this first census took place, Quirinius was the governor of Syria. Everyone then, went to register himself, each to his own town. Joseph

went from the town of Nazareth in Galilee to the town of Bethlehem in Judea, the birthplace of King David. Joseph went there because he was a descendant of David. He went to register with Mary, who was promised in marriage to him. She was pregnant, and while they were in Bethlehem, the time came for her to have her baby. She gave birth to her first son, wrapped him in strips of cloth and laid him in a manger—there was no room for them to stay in the inn.

The general census at the time of the Nativity corresponds to mass education at the time Barack Obama was born, and the registration of Joseph and Mary in Bethlehem corresponds to the matriculation of Barack Obama (father) and Stanley Ann Dunham. In fact, when Barack Obama was born, both his father and his mother were studying at the University of Hawaii in Honolulu.

There appears to be a disagreement here, because Honolulu in Hawaii was not the city of origin of Barack Obama Sr. as Bethlehem in Judea was the city of origin of Joseph—the birthplace of King David. The logic is that in the Diaspora the true city of every Jew is not the city of David but his or her own place of residence. Moreover, with the coming of the Messiah Jesus Christ the "chosen" ones are no longer Jews only, but Gentiles as well. In Galatians 3:13–14, the scriptures say,

> But by becoming a curse for us Christ has redeemed us from the curse that the Law brings, for the scripture says, "Anyone who is hanged on a tree is under God's curse." Christ did this in order that the blessing which God promised to Abraham might be given to the Gentiles by means of Christ Jesus, so that through faith we might receive the Spirit promised by God.

The education of Barack Obama Sr. and Stanley Ann Dunham gave them knowledge and, hence, civilization and power. This is affirmed in Romans 2:28–29, where it is written,

> After all, who is a real Jew, truly circumcised? It is not the man who is a Jew on the outside, whose circumcision is a physical thing. Rather, the real Jew is a person who is a Jew on the inside, that is, whose heart has been circumcised, and this is the work of God's Spirit, not of the written Law. Such a person receives praise from God, not from human beings.

And in Hebrews 13:14, it is written, "For there is no permanent city for us here on earth; we are looking for the city which is to come."

Therefore, being a foreign student in the United States of America at that time, the father of Barack Obama was one of the "chosen" Gentiles. His city was the University of Hawaii in Honolulu where he was studying. This conforms with the scriptures in Isaiah 56:6–8:

> And the Lord says to those foreigners who become part of his people, who love him and serve him, who observe the Sabbath and faithfully keep his covenant: "I will bring you to Zion, my sacred hill, give you joy in my house of prayer, and accept the sacrifices you offer on my altar. My temple will be called a house of prayer for the people of all nations." The Sovereign Lord, who has brought his people Israel home from exile, has promised that he will bring still other people to join them.

These scriptures are fulfilled in the vast melting pot of the United States of America, where, in principle, everyone has the right to come to live and work.

We will now examine the similarities between Barack Obama and Jesus Christ. Then we will confirm that the birth, childhood, revelation, victory, and accession of Barack Obama to the White House all constitute a replay of the Nativity, revelation, crucifixion, resurrection, and ascension of Jesus Christ into heaven.

From Two Different Worlds

First, like the parents of Jesus Christ, the parents of Barack Obama were of two different natures. Stanley Ann Dunham was a white American, while Barack Hussein Obama Sr. was a black African. This is in agreement with the belief that Jesus Christ was conceived by God the Holy Spirit and born of a human being—the Virgin Mary. This is written in the scriptures in Luke 1:30–31, 34–35:

> The angel said to her, "Don't be afraid, Mary, God had been gracious to you. You will become pregnant and give birth to a son, and you will name him Jesus." Mary said to the angel, "I am a virgin. How, then, can this be?" The angel answered, "The Holy Spirit will come on you, and God's power will rest upon you. For this reason the holy child will be called the Son of God."

Also, in Matthew 1:19–21 the scripture says,

> Joseph was a man, who always did what was right, but he did not want to disgrace Mary publicly, so he made plans to break the engagement privately. While he was thinking about this, an angel of

the Lord appeared to him in a dream and said,
"Joseph, descendant of David, do not be afraid to
take Mary to be your wife. For it is by the Holy
Spirit that she has conceived. She will have a son,
and you will name him Jesus—because he will
save his people from their sins."

Second, like the parents of Jesus Christ, the parents of
Barack Obama were from two different origins. Thus, as the
Holy Spirit came from heaven and Mary from the earth, so
Barack Obama Sr. came from Africa and Stanley Ann Dunham
from America. The only difference is that in the case of Jesus
Christ the father came from above and the mother from below,
whereas in the case of Barack Obama the mother came from
above and the father from below. It was so, certainly, because
by their levels of civilization the United States was similar to
heaven while Kenya in Africa was similar to the earth.

The Manger[12]

Third, the birth of Barack Obama was like the Nativity
of Jesus Christ. In Luke 2:7 it is written, "She [Mary] gave
birth to her first son, wrapped him in strips of cloth, and laid
him in a manger—there was no room for them to stay in the
inn." The manger, here, has a triple similarity to the place and
conditions of the birth of Barack Obama.

Barack Obama was born in Hawaii, the fiftieth and last
state of the United States. The size and location of Hawaii in
the Pacific Ocean off the mainland of the United States makes
it, in fact, a "manger." Besides, Barack Obama was brought
up in foster homes because his parents divorced, and there
was "no room for them"—that is, the father, mother, and
son—in the matrimonial home. Also, the foster home—the
small apartment of his maternal grandparents in Hawaii—was

a "manger" compared to the "inn" that was the home of his mother and father.

Furthermore, the biography of Barack Obama reveals that during the few years that he lived with his mother and stepfather in Jakarta in Indonesia, he was exposed to glaring scenes of poverty. Indonesia, at that time, was a "manger" compared to the United States, with her abundant wealth and advanced civilization.

Fourth, like Jesus Christ, Barack Obama was the firstborn and the only son to both his father and his mother. It is recorded that Barack Obama was born to Barack Obama Sr. and Stanley Ann Dunham, who were both young students at the University of Hawaii and who were married from 1960 to 1965. It is also reported that Barack Obama has one half sister, Maya, who was born to his mother and stepfather in 1970. These two facts agree with what is written in the scriptures about Jesus Christ. In Luke 1:7, the scripture say, "She [Mary] gave birth to her first son, wrapped him in strips of cloth, and laid him in a manger—there was no room for them to stay in the inn." Then, in John 1:14, it is written, "The Word became a human being and, full of grace and truth, lived among us. We saw his glory, the glory which he received as the Father's only Son."

The Foster Fathers

Fifth, both Barack Obama and Jesus Christ were brought up by foster fathers. Barack Obama was conceived by Barack Obama Sr. and fathered by his maternal grandfather—Mr. Dunham. This is similar to the fact that Jesus Christ was conceived by the Holy Spirit and fathered by Joseph, to whom Mary was promised in marriage. Thus the scripture says in Matthew 1:18, "This was how the birth of Jesus Christ took place. His mother, Mary, was engaged to Joseph, but before they were married, she found out that she was going to have a baby by the Holy Spirit." Also, in Luke 3:23, the scripture says, "When Jesus began his work, he was about thirty years old. He was the son, so people thought of Joseph, who was the son of Heli." Jesus Christ, himself, confirmed that God was his true father when Joseph and Mary went to look for him in the temple in Jerusalem. This is written in Luke 2:45–51:

> They did not find him, so they went back to Jerusalem looking for him. On the third day they found him in the temple, sitting with Jewish teachers, listening to them and asking questions. All who heard him were amazed at his intelligent answers. His parents were astonished when they saw him, and his mother said to him, "My son, why have you done this to us? Your father and I have been terribly worried trying to find you." He answered them, "Why did you have to look for me? Didn't you know that I had to be in my Father's house?" But they did not understand his answer. So Jesus went back with them to Nazareth, where he was obedient to them. His mother treasured all these things in her heart.

The sixth relationship between Barack Obama and Jesus Christ is that their foster fathers both made their living from wood. Mr. Dunham was a furniture salesman—very similar to Joseph, who was a carpenter. The fact that Joseph was a carpenter is revealed by the scriptures in Matthew 13:53–56, where it is written,

> When Jesus finished telling these parables, he left that place and went back to his hometown. He taught in the synagogue, and those who heard him were amazed. "Where did he get such wisdom?" they asked. "And what about his miracles? Isn't he the carpenter's son? Isn't Mary

his mother, and aren't James, Joseph, Simon, and Judas his brothers? Aren't all his sisters living here? Where did he get all this?"

The Flight to Egypt

The seventh similarity between Barack Obama and Jesus Christ is that each of them, in his childhood, was taken to a foreign country for safety. It is reported that the father of Barack Obama returned to Kenya alone and that his mother married an Indonesian oil manager and moved to Jakarta when Barack Obama was six years old. This corresponds to what the scriptures say in Matthew 2:14–15 about Jesus Christ: "Joseph got up, took the child and his mother and left during the night for Egypt, where he stayed until Herod died. This was done to make what the Lord had said through the prophet come true, 'I called my Son out of Egypt.'" Thus, the stepfather of Barack Obama took him to Indonesia as Joseph took Jesus Christ to Egypt. However, Barack Obama was not taken away to Indonesia because someone wanted to kill him as Herod wanted to kill Jesus Christ, but because he was too young to be left behind.

The Sword of Herod

Notwithstanding, history reports that when Barack Obama was born, a gunman was hunting for the president of the United States of America just as Herod was looking for the King of the Jews, Jesus Christ, to kill him. Thus, on November 22, 1963, in Dallas, Texas,[13] the famous American president, John Fitzgerald Kennedy, was assassinated. It was two years after he took office and two years after the birth of Barack Obama—what a fascinating correspondence! The assassination of John Kennedy agreed with what the scriptures say in Matthew 2:16–18:

> When Herod realized that the visitors from the east had tricked him, he was furious. He gave orders to kill all the boys in Bethlehem and its neighborhood who were two years old and younger—this was done in accordance with what he had learned from the visitors about the time when the star had appeared. In this way what the prophet Jeremiah had said came true: "A sound is heard in Ramah, the sound of bitter weeping. Rachel is crying for her children, she refuses to be comforted, for they are dead."

There are three similarities that come out very clearly from these scriptures. The first one is that the visitors from the east deceived Herod and made it impossible for him to kill Jesus Christ. In the same way, the Indonesian oil manager married the mother of Barack Obama and took them to Jakarta—though, when John Kennedy was assassinated, Barack Obama and his parents were still living in the United States. The second one is that Herod killed all the boys in Bethlehem who were two years old and younger. Similarly, John Fitzgerald Kennedy was killed in his second year in office, and at that time Barack Obama was also two years of age. The last one is that in Ramah there was the sound of bitter weeping; Rachel was crying for her dead children, and she refused to be comforted. In fact, every American wept when John Kennedy was brutally shot down in the company of his wife, and the United States and the rest of the world still have not stopped mourning him. This is evidenced by the many memorials erected in the United States and other countries of the world in honor of the eminent statesman. In fact, no deceased American president, so far, has received the homage paid to John Kennedy.

Chicago and Nazareth

The eighth similarity between Barack Obama and Jesus Christ is that each of them eventually took residence in a place different from where he was born. Barack Obama settled in Chicago, Illinois, instead of in Honolulu, Hawaii, where he was born. In fact, it was from Illinois that he was elected to the US Senate, from where he eventually won his ticket to the White House. This is in agreement with the fact that when Jesus Christ was brought back from Egypt, Joseph took him to live in Nazareth instead of Bethlehem, where he was born. This is written in Matthew 2:21–23: "So Joseph got up, took the child and his mother, and went back to Israel. He was given more instructions in a dream, so he went to the province of Galilee and made his home in a town named Nazareth. And so what the prophets had said came true: 'He will be called a Nazarene.'" So, it also happened that Barack Obama was revealed from the city of Chicago, where God inspired him to live.

The Significance of the Manger

It is obvious that if Barack Obama had been born and bred in one of the stable and luxurious homes of the United States, he would not have gained the profound humanity that, together with his unbending audacity, has made him the symbol of change and hope. Thus the scriptures say in Matthew 2:4–6,

> He called together all the chief priests and the teachers of the Law and asked them, "Where will the Messiah be born?" "In the town of Bethlehem in Judea," they answered. "For this is what the Prophet wrote: 'Bethlehem in the Land of Judah,

you are by no means the least of the leading cities of Judah; for from you will come a leader who will guide my people Israel.'"

Therefore, the election of Barack Obama as the forty-fourth president of the United States of America fulfills the Word of God that was announced in 1 Peter 2:6–9:

For the scripture says: "I chose a valuable stone, which I am placing as the cornerstone in Zion; and whoever believes in him will never be disappointed." This stone is of great value for you that believe; but for those who do not believe: "The stone which the builders rejected as worthless turned out to be the most important of all."

And another scripture says: "This is the stone that will make people stumble, the rock that will make them fall. They stumbled because they did not believe in the word; such was God's will for them. But you are the chosen race, the King's priests, the holy nation, God's own people, chosen to proclaim the wonderful acts of God, who called you out of darkness into his own marvelous light."

In fact, the election of Barack Obama was a divine gift to edify the human race through freedom, justice, and equality. And this fulfills the scriptures in James 1:17–18, where it is written,

Every good gift and every perfect present comes from heaven; it comes down from God, the Creator of the heavenly lights, who does not change or cause darkness by turning. By his own will he brought us into being through the word

of truth, so that we should have first place among
all his creatures.

Conclusion

These facts lead us to the unquestionable conclusion that
Barack Obama is not an ordinary human being, although he
is not Jesus the Christ. They prove that he is a special person
to whom God has given a special duty. Thus his election into
the White House was mysteriously calculated and ordered in
time to fulfill that divine purpose. There can be no claim to
the contrary, because the particular circumstances of his birth
and upbringing only brought Barack Obama into the reality of
the world that time and destiny were to elect him as its leader.
Thus, in Micah 5:1–5, the scriptures say,

> People of Jerusalem gather your forces! We are
> besieged! They are attacking the leader of Israel.
> The Lord says, "Bethlehem Ephrata, you are one
> of the smallest towns in Judah but out of you I
> will bring a ruler for Israel, whose family line goes
> back to ancient times." So the Lord will abandon
> his people to their enemies until the woman who
> is to give birth has her son. Then those Israelites
> who are in exile will be reunited with their own
> people. When he comes he will rule his people
> with the strength that comes from the Lord and
> with the majesty of the Lord God himself. His
> people will live in safety because people all over
> the earth will acknowledge his greatness, and he
> will bring peace.

Therefore, God chose Barack Obama from the small city
of Honolulu in Hawaii to rule the United States, just as he
chose Jesus Christ from the small town of Bethlehem in Judea

to rule Israel. And, in fact, the greatness of Barack Obama has already been recognized by the world, judging from the jubilation that followed his election on November 4, 2008. Besides, Barack Obama was awarded the Nobel Peace Prize in 2009—only one year into his first term as president of the United States. Since his first inauguration, his diplomatic influence has continued to increase and affect the politics of the world.

In chapter 2, we will examine the signs in the life of Barack Obama that are similar to the messianic signs of Jesus Christ.

---

12. A **manger** is an open box for feeding animals such as goats, sheep, and cattle. It symbolizes a common, mean, or unimportant place.

13. Bill O'Reilly and Martin Dugard, *Killing Lincoln: The Shocking Assassination That Changed America Forever* (New York: Henry Holt & Co., 2011).

†

Artwork 3 of 21: Cross. This is the symbol of
selflessness, redemption, and life after death.

CHAPTER TWO

The Signs of the Messiah

> When he comes, he will rule his people with
> the strength that comes from the Lord and
> with the majesty of the Lord God himself. His
> people will live in safety because people all
> over the earth will acknowledge his greatness,
> and he will bring peace.
>
> (Micah 5:4–5)

THE phenomenon of life after death is not excluded from the world of ordinary experience. The germination of a seed perfectly reveals and confirms the fact that something or someone must die in order to give life to another.

The Seed and the Shoot

When a seed is planted in the soil, it stays dormant until atmospheric conditions make it germinate. When this happens, the leaves and the roots begin to grow and draw food from the seed. Finally, the seed withers and dies when the roots penetrate the soil and the leaves and stem shoot out of the ground. This natural process simply demonstrates the mystery of life after death as it is written in Corinthians 15:36–38: "You fool! When you sow a seed in the ground, it does not sprout to life unless it dies. And what you sow is a bare seed, perhaps a grain of wheat or some other grains, not the full-bodied plant that will later grow up. God provides that seed with the body He wishes; He gives each seed its own proper body."

Besides, in John 12:24–25, the scriptures say, "I am telling you the truth: a grain of wheat remains no more than a single grain unless it is dropped into the ground and dies. If it does die, then it produces many grains. Those who love their own life will lose it; those who hate their own life in this world will keep it for life eternal." This means that one must die in the body and live in the spirit to experience true life on earth. In other words, for anyone to arise and shine like the sun (Isaiah 60:1), the substance of that one must die to liberate the essence.

Madelyn Dunham and Barack Obama

It is but in this context that we may interpret the death of Madelyn Dunham—the maternal grandmother of Barack Obama. She died in Hawaii on Monday, November 3, 2008—the eve of her grandson's election as president of the United States. It is known that Madelyn Dunham was both the foster mother and the mentor of Barack Obama. For this reason, he paid her tribute on several occasions, acknowledging her as the provider of his education and the architect of his virtues. The last time he paid her respect was two weeks before her death, when Barack Obama left his campaign trail to see Madelyn Dunham on her sickbed in Hawaii.

Thus, the seed, Madelyn Dunham, withered and died for Barack Obama to shoot into the limelight. Evidently,

Barack Obama tapped the spirit of Madelyn Dunham to firmly implant himself and rise above the expectations of everyone. In a way, Madelyn Dunham died, but her essence lives and triumphs in Barack Obama. May her soul rest in peace! But unanswered questions remain: One—Why did Madelyn Dunham die only at the eve of the historic victory of Barack Obama? Two—Did Madelyn Dunham die for her grandson to win the 2008 presidential election? Three—Did Barack Obama win the 2008 presidential election because his grandmother died? The answers to these questions are hard to find, but it comes out clearly that the death of Madelyn Dunham and the election of Barack Obama correspond to three biblical mysteries.

Moses and Joshua

The first correspondence is that the death of Madelyn Dunham and the election of Barack Obama were like the death of Moses and the appointment of Joshua to lead the people of Israel into the Promised Land. In Deuteronomy 34:4–9, it is written,

> Then the Lord said to Moses, "This is the land that I promised Abraham, Isaac, and Jacob I would give to their descendants. I have let you see it, but I will not let you go there." So Moses, the Lord's servant, died there in the land of Moab, as the Lord had said he would. The Lord buried him in a valley in Moab, opposite the town of Bethpeor, but to this day no one knows the exact place of his burial. Moses was 120 years old when he died; he was as strong as ever, and his eyesight was still good. The people of Israel mourned for him for thirty days in the plains of Moab. Joshua, son of Nun, was filled with wisdom, because

> Moses had appointed him to be his successor.
> The people of Israel obeyed Joshua and kept the
> commandments that the Lord had given them
> through Moses.

Thus, Moses led the Israelites out of slavery in the land of Egypt, through forty years of wandering and suffering in the desert, but he died without reaching the Promised Land—although he stood and saw it with his own eyes. In the same way, Madelyn Dunham brought Barack Obama out of "slavery" in Indonesia and mentored him for forty years—he was six years old when he came back from Jakarta, and he began his campaign for the White House in 2007 at the age of forty-six. Forty-six minus six is equal to forty. In fact, Madelyn Dunham saw Barack Obama rising to the presidency, but she did not see him in the White House.

John the Baptist and Jesus Christ

The second correspondence is that the death of Madelyn Dunham and the election of Barack Obama were like the death of John the Baptist and the revelation of Jesus Christ. In Matthew 3:11, 13, and 16, it is written, "'I [John the Baptist] baptize you with water to show that you have repented, but the one who will come after me will baptize you with the Holy Spirit and fire. He is much greater than I am; and I am not good enough even to carry his sandals.' At that time Jesus arrived from Galilee and came to John at the Jordan to be baptized by him. As soon as Jesus was baptized, he came up out of the water. Then heaven was opened to him, and he saw the Spirit of God coming down like a dove and alighting on him." And in Matthew 11:10–11, Jesus says, "For John is the one of whom the scripture says, 'God said, I will send my messenger ahead of you to open the way for you.' I assure you that John the Baptist is greater than anyone who had ever lived, but the one who is least in the kingdom of heaven is greater than John."

Furthermore, in John 3:25–30, it is written,

> Some of John's disciples began arguing with a Jew about the matter of ritual washing. So they went to John and said, "Teacher, you remember the man who was with you on the east side of the Jordan, the one you spoke about? Well, he is baptizing now, and everyone is going to him!" John answered, "No one can have anything unless God gives it to him. You yourselves are my witnesses that I said, 'I am not the Messiah, but I have been sent ahead of him.' The bridegroom is the one to whom the bride belongs, but the bridegroom's friend, who stands by and listens, is glad when he hears the bridegroom's voice. This is how my own happiness is made complete. He [Jesus] must become more important while I become less important."

The scriptures further reveal that John the Baptist was thrown into prison and eventually killed. And it is important to note that when Jesus heard about the imprisonment of John the Baptist, he did nothing about it, because it was to fulfill the scriptures. Thus, in Matthew 4:12–17, it is written,

> When Jesus heard that John had been put in prison, he went away to Galilee. He did not stay in Nazareth but went to live in Capernaum, a town by Lake Galilee, in the territory of Zebulun and Naphtali. This was done to make what the prophet Isaiah had said come true: "Land of Zebulun and land of Naphtali, on the road to the

sea, on the other side of the Jordan, Galilee; land of the Gentiles! The people who live in darkness will see a great light. On those who live in the dark land of death the light will shine." From that time Jesus began to preach his message: "Turn away from your sins, because the kingdom of heaven is near!"

Then, in Matthew 14:3–4, 10, and 12, the scriptures say,

For Herod had earlier ordered John's arrest and he had him chained and put in prison. He had done this because of Herodias, his brother Philip's wife. For some time John the Baptist had told Herod, "It isn't right for you to be married to Herodias!" So he had John beheaded in prison. John's disciples came, carried away his body, and buried it; then they went and told Jesus.

But what is very striking is that when John the Baptist died, Jesus went on to perform many miracles. Thus it is written in Matthew 14:13–14, "When Jesus heard the news about John [the news of his death], he left there in a boat and went to a lonely place by himself. The people heard about it, so they left their towns and followed him by land. Jesus got out of the boat, and when he saw the large crowd, his heart was filled with pity for them, and he healed those who were ill." In Matthew 14:19–21, the scripture says,

He ordered the people to sit down on the grass; then he took the five loaves and the two fish, looked up to heaven, and gave thanks to God. He broke the loaves and gave them to the disciples, and the disciples gave them to the people. Everyone ate and had enough. Then the disciples took up twelve baskets full of what was left over. The number of men who ate was about five thousand, not counting the women and children.

Then, in Matthew 14:25–26, it is written, "Between three and six o' clock in the morning Jesus came to the disciples, walking on the water. When they saw him walking on the water, they were terrified. 'It's a ghost!' they said, and screamed with fear." And in Mark 4:36–40, the scriptures say,

> So they left the crowd; the disciples got into the boat in which Jesus was already sitting, and they took him with them. Other boats were there too. Suddenly a strong wind blew up, and the waves began to spill over into the boat, so that it was about to fill with water. Jesus was in the back of the boat, sleeping with his head on a pillow. The disciples woke him up and said, "Teacher, don't you care that we are about to die?" Jesus stood up and commanded the wind, "Be quiet!" and he said to the waves, "Be still!" The wind died down, and there was a great calm. Then Jesus said to his disciples, "Why are you frightened? Have you still no faith?"

Ascension and Pentecost

The third correspondence is that the death of Madelyn Dunham and the election of Barack Obama were like the death of Jesus Christ and the coming of the Holy Spirit. In Galatians 3:13–14, it is written, "By becoming a curse for us Christ has redeemed us from the curse that the Law brings; for the scripture says, 'Anyone who is hanged on a tree is under God's curse.' Christ did this in order that the blessing which

God promised to Abraham might be given to the Gentiles by means of Christ Jesus, so that through faith we might receive the Spirit promised by God." Furthermore, in Hebrews 9:15–18, the scripture says,

> For this reason Christ is the one who arranges a new covenant, so that those who have been called by God may receive the eternal blessings that God has promised. This can be done because there has been a death which sets people free from the wrongs they did while the first covenant was in force. In the case of a will it is necessary to prove that the person who made it has died, for a will means nothing while the person who made it is alive; it comes to effect only after his death. That is why even the first covenant came into effect only with the use of blood.

Finally, in John 16:7, Jesus Christ says, "But I am telling you the truth: it is better for you that I go away, because if I do not go, the Helper (Holy Spirit) will not come to you. But if I do go away, then I will send him to you."

These mysteries, in fact, mark Barack Obama with the signs of the Messiah—Jesus Christ. The correspondences prove that his election to the White House was mysteriously calculated to happen in both time and space. Besides, they stand out to confirm the divine ordination of Barack Obama as a messiah to America and the whole world in the twenty-first century.

Simeon and the Child Jesus

Therefore, it would be wrong to think that Madelyn Dunham regretted dying at the time she did or that it was unfortunate for her to die without seeing Barack Obama in the

White House. In fact, she must have just been as grateful as the old man Simeon. Thus the scriptures say in Luke 2:25–32,

> At that time there was a man named Simeon living in Jerusalem. He was a good, God-fearing man and was waiting for Israel to be saved. The Holy Spirit was with him and had assured him that he would not die before he had seen the Lord's promised Messiah. Led by the Spirit, Simeon went into the temple. When the parents brought the child Jesus into the temple to do for him what the Law required, Simeon took the child in his arms and gave thanks to God: "Now, Lord, you have kept your promise, and you may let your servant go in peace. With my own eyes I have seen your salvation which you have prepared in the presence of all peoples: a light to reveal your will to the Gentiles and bring glory to your people Israel."

And who knows if at the hour of her death she was not singing the song of the Blessed Virgin Mary as it is written in Luke 1:46–55:

> My heart praises the Lord; my soul is glad because of God my Savior, for he has remembered me, his lowly servant! From now on all people will call me happy, because of the great things the Mighty God has done for me. His name is holy; from one generation to another he shows mercy to those who honor him. He has stretched out his mighty arm and scattered the proud with all their plans. He has brought down mighty kings from their thrones, and lifted up the lowly. He has filled the hungry with good things, and sent the rich away with empty hands. He has kept the promise he

made to our ancestors, and has come to the help of his servant Israel. He has remembered to show mercy to Abraham and to all his descendants forever!

In chapter 3, we examine the number one as a vital number of Barack Obama.

Artwork 4 of 21: Dot and Circle. This is the symbol of originality, creativity, and authority.

CHAPTER THREE

The Mysteries of One

> Fling wide the gates, open the ancient doors
> and the great king will come in. Who is this
> king? He is the Lord, strong and mighty, the
> Lord, victorious in battle.
>
> (Psalm 24:7–8)

THE number one is numerically written as 1, and it is graphically represented by a dot in a circle.

The Signs of the Number One

Before examining the symbolism of the number one and the role it plays in the life and activities of Barack Obama, let us first determine whether the number one is one of his vital numbers. Accordingly, the following facts are presented as signs that identify Barack Obama with the number one.

1. On June 3, 2008, Barack Obama won the Montana Democratic Party primary against Hillary Clinton, which gave him enough delegates to become the first African American to win a major political party's nomination for the office of president of the United States. Here, the fact that he was the first-ever black presidential nominee in the United States automatically identifies him with the number one.

2. The numerical reduction of the date of June 3, 2008, when Barack Obama won the Montana primary and the Democratic Party nomination for the presidency of the United States is equal to the number one. When we calculate $6 + 3 + 2 + 0 + 0 + 8 = 19 = 1 + 9 = 10 = 1 + 0 = 1$, we obtain the number one.

3. In 2008 Barack Obama ran for president and won, becoming the first African American ever to be elected to the White House. Besides being the first African American to be elected president, he was elected in the year 2008. His position as the first African American president of the United States identifies Barack Obama with the number one. Also, the numerical reduction of 2008 is equal to the number one. When we calculate $2 + 0 + 0 + 8 = 10 = 1 + 0 = 1$, we obtain the number one.

4. In 1990 Barack Obama became the first African American editor of the *Harvard Law Review* of Harvard University. His chronological position as the first African American editor of the *Harvard Law Review* identifies him with the number one. Also, the numerical reduction of 1990 is equal to the number one. When we calculate $1 + 9 + 9 + 0 = 19 = 1 + 9 = 10 = 1 + 0 = 1$, we obtain the number one.

5. Barack Obama was the first American president to be born in the state of Hawaii. This fact identifies him with the number one.

6. It is reported that after the separation of his parents in 1965 Barack Obama was visited by his father only once—and when he was ten years old. The fact that his father visited him only once identifies him with the number one. Also, the numerical reduction of his age, ten years at that time, is equal to the number one. When we calculate $1 + 0 = 1$, we obtain the number one.

7. Barack Obama has only one half sister, Maya, who was born to his mother and stepfather in 1970. This fact also identifies him with the number one.

8. Barack Obama was the first child who was born to his parents, and the only boy born to either of them. These two facts identify him with the number one.

9. At school Barack Obama had four nicknames, and one of them was "The One." This proves that from childhood he already expressed his identity with the number one.

10. Barack Obama was born in 1961, which was the first year of that decade. This fact identifies him with the number one.

Thus we can confirm without any doubt that the life and activities of Barack Obama are intimately associated with the number one. Therefore, the number one is one of his vital numbers.

The Symbolisms of the Number One

Having made certain that Barack Obama is truly associated with the number one, we will proceed to discuss the symbolism of the number one.

1. The number one is the symbol of creativity because it represents God—the Creator of the universe and the source of life. In geometry the number one is represented by a dot, which is the origin, or beginning. When the dot is enclosed in a circle, it stands for God as the ruler of the universe. Thus, in Genesis 1:1–2, the scriptures say, "In the beginning, when God created the universe, the earth was formless and desolate. The raging ocean that covered everything was engulfed in total darkness, and the Spirit of God was moving over the water."

2. The number one is the symbol of originality because it is the origin of everything.

3. The number one is the symbol of initiative because it is the beginning of everything. It is essential to the formation and existence of all other numbers because they all originate from and depend on it.

4. The number one is the symbol of supremacy. In arithmetic it is the least, but in order of merit it is the highest and most powerful number.

5. The number one is the symbol of excellence. In arithmetic it is the least, but in order of merit it is the first and best of all numbers.

6. The number one is the symbol of unity because it contains everything. The number one symbolizes the ego, the "I" or "I am." It always comes first; it is different from the rest and sometimes has the tendency to exclude others. The number one is, therefore, both independent and selfish. But for the sake of coexistence and its desire to dominate, it propagates and accommodates all other numbers.

7. The number one is the symbol of integrity because it unites everything.

8. The number one is the symbol of eternity because any number that is divided or multiplied by one remains the same.

9. The number one is the symbol of infinity because the progressive addition of one to nothing yields an infinite number.

10. The number one is the symbol of particularity because anything that is one has no pair.

11. The number one symbolizes the center from which all things and power emanate. It is the symbol of leadership and supremacy. In nature, the number one symbolizes the gene or seed of reproduction that is inherent in all living things. And in outer space the number one stands for the sun, which is the center of the solar system and the source of its light and energy.

The Power of the Number One

By virtue of its symbolism, the number one, as a weapon, has the following merits:

1. The number one has the power to initiate, to create, or to innovate. It is spontaneous because it can propagate itself at will. When we calculate 1 + 1 = 2, we obtain two; 2 + 1 = 3, we obtain three; and so forth—the trend is unlimited.

2. The number one has the wisdom to lead or to guide. It is all-knowing because it understands all numbers.

3. The number one has the power to unite, to integrate, or to combine. It is ever-present because it is contained in all other numbers.

4. The number one has the power to overcome, to dominate, and to rule. It is all-powerful because it surpasses all other numbers.

5. The number one has the power to confiscate and to exclude. It is sovereign and independent because it depends only on itself and so can exist alone.

The question now is, How does the number one, as a weapon, enable Barack Obama to win and exercise power in the White House?

1. The number one enabled Barack Obama to conceive the idea of vying for the presidency of the United States of America. In fact, when he announced his intention in 2006 to enter the competition for the White House, it was rather impulsive—and many observers took it as a joke. However, when he won the 2008 Democratic Party nomination for the presidency, his horizons began to brighten. Finally, on November 4, 2008, the sun shone on him, and it shone again on November 6, 2012—and each time it came as a surprise.

2. The number one enabled Barack Obama to conceive a particular political idea—Change We Need, Change We Can Believe In.

3. The number one enabled Barack Obama to excel, to lead, and to surpass all his rivals.

4. The number one enabled Barack Obama to dominate and to overpower his adversaries.

5. The number one enabled Barack Obama to integrate the different races and groups of people in the United States to support his political platform for change.

6. The number one enabled Barack Obama to rally and organize a great number of volunteers into efficient and effective campaign and monitoring teams.

7. The number one enabled Barack Obama to attract funds and collect a huge sum of $605 million to finance his 2008 presidential campaign.

8. The number one enables Barack Obama to boost his power, magnetism, and popularity at all times to obtain victory. In fact, the great magnetism, creativity, excellence, oratory, and faith that characterize President Barack Obama are all attributes of the number one—the Spirit of God.

9. The number one enables Barack Obama to instantly disprove accusations, challenge his opponents, and win political debates.

10. The number one enables Barack Obama to isolate and distinguish himself as a competent, courageous, and dependable leader.

11. The number one enables Barack Obama to reject the status quo and to propose change for the United States and the whole world.

12. The number one enables Barack Obama to impose his ideas, decisions, and plans on the political scenes at home and abroad.

13. The number one enables Barack Obama to surpass all his rivals and to gain power.

14. The number one gives Barack Obama unlimited creativity and initiative to propose solutions to the problems of the United States and the world today.

15. The number one enables Barack Obama to integrate the different races and classes of people in the United States into a more united and stronger nation.

16. The number one enables Barack Obama to reinvent the American dream and to forge a better world order. In fact, there are clear signs that his second term will leave very strong legacies of change, the foundations of which were laid in his first term. These would include social justice, universal health care, economic recovery, unity in diversity, human liberties, world peace, and the control of guns and climate change. Thus, in his second inaugural speech Barack Obama said, "A decade of war is ending and economic recovery has begun," "America's possibilities are limitless," "Diversity and openness are the two great resources which America has," and "Americans must come together to seize the moment."[14]

17. The number one will enable Barack Obama to rule America for the maximum possible length of time—which is eight years.

In chapter 4, we will examine the number two as a vital number of Barack Obama.

---

14. BBC World News, January 21, 2013.

Artwork 5 of 21: Straight Line Linking Two Points. This is the symbol of loyalty, attraction, and unity.

CHAPTER FOUR

The Mysteries of Two

> And we have seen and tell others that the Father sent his Son to be the Savior of the world. If anyone declares that Jesus is the Son of God, he lives in union with God and God lives in union with him.
>
> (1 John 4:14)

THE number two is numerically written as 2. It is the first mathematical extension of the number one. When we calculate 1 + 1 = 2, we obtain the number two. The number two is graphically represented by a straight line linking two points together.

The Signs of the Number Two

There is abundant evidence that identifies Barack Obama with the number two. The following numerical reductions prove that the number two is a vital number of Barack Obama.

1. The name "Barack Obama," as the name "Jesus Christ," has eleven characters. The numerical reduction of eleven is equal to the number two. When we calculate 11 = 1 + 1 = 2, we obtain the number two.

2. His full name, Barack Hussein Obama Jr., has twenty letters. The numerical reduction of twenty is equal to the number two. When we calculate 20 = 2 + 0 = 2, we obtain the number two.

3. Barack Obama was born on August 4, 1961. The numerical reduction of August four nineteen sixty-one is equal to the number two. When we calculate $(0 + 8) + (0 + 4) + (1 + 9 + 6 + 1) = 4 + 8 + 17 = 4 + 8 + 1 + 7 = 20 = 2 + 0 = 2$, we obtain the number two.

4. Barack Obama was forty-seven years old when he was first elected president of the United States in 2008. The numerical reduction of forty-seven is equal to the number two. When we calculate $47 = 4 + 7 = 11 = 1 + 1 = 2$, we obtain the number two.

5. Barack Obama became US senator from Illinois on January 3, 2005. The numerical reduction of January three two thousand and five is equal to the number two. When we calculate $(0 + 1) + (0 + 3) + (2 + 0 + 0 + 5) = 3 + 1 + 7 = 11 = 1 + 1 = 2$, we obtain the number two.

6. Barack Obama raised the enormous sum of $605 million in 2008 to finance his presidential campaign. The numerical reduction of six hundred and five million is equal to the number two. When we calculate $6 + 0 + 5 + 0 + 0 + 0 + 0 + 0 + 0 = 11 = 1 + 1 = 2$, we obtain the number two.

7. On January 20, 2009, Barack Obama took the oath of office in the presence of two million people in Washington, DC. The numerical reduction of two million is equal to the number two. When we calculate 2 + 0 + 0 + 0 + 0 + 0 + 0 = 2, we obtain the number two.

8. The parents of Barack Obama had two different colors—black and white. They came from two different countries—Kenya and the United States. They also came from two different continents—Africa and North America. These are all signs of the number two.

9. Barack Obama was brought up in two different homes—his stepfather's home in Jakarta and his maternal grandmother's home in Hawaii. He grew up in two different countries—Indonesia and the United States; and in two different continents—Asia and North America. These are more signs of the number two.

10. Barack and Michelle Obama have two children—Malia and Sasha. This is a sign of the number two.

11. Barack Obama is one of the two children of his mother. His half sister, Maya, was born to his mother and stepfather in 1970. This is a sign of the number two.

12. On January 21, 2013, Barack Obama took his second oath of office with his left hand placed on two Bibles—one that was used by Abraham Lincoln and another that was used by Martin Luther King Jr. This is another sign of the number two.

The Symbolism of the Number Two

Before discussing how Barack Obama uses the holy weapon of the number two to win and exercise power in the White House, we will first examine the symbolism of the number two.

1. The number two represents the duality of nature or the two sexes of male and female, which make reproduction possible. It symbolizes the reproduction and multiplication of species. The number two also represents the propagation of a plant from the seed and, hence, growth and expansion.

2. The number two represents the positive (+) and negative (-) polarities, which combine to produce magnetism and electricity.

3. The number two symbolizes affinity and relationship. These include friendship, marriage, and the association of people and groups of people for any purpose.

4. The number two also symbolizes opposition and divergence, as well as revolution and change.

5. The number two is the symbol of Jesus Christ, who is the second person of the Holy Trinity.

6. The number two symbolizes the incarnation of God as man in the person of Jesus Christ. Thus, in John 1:1, 2, 4, 14, and 18, it is written,

> In the beginning the Word already existed; the Word was with God, and the Word was God. From the very beginning the Word was with God. The Word

was the source of life, and this life brought light to humanity. The Word became a human being and, full of grace and truth, lived among us. We saw his glory, the glory that he received as the Father's only Son. No one has ever seen God. The only Son, who is the same as God and is at the Father's side, has made him known.

7. The number two symbolizes Jesus Christ as the Messiah and the only Son of God. In John 3:16–17, the scriptures say, "For God loved the world so much that he gave his only Son, so that everyone who believes in Him may not die but have eternal life. For God did not send his Son into the world to be its judge, but to be its Savior."

The Power of the Number Two

As a weapon the number two has the following powers:

1. The number two has the power to expand and to multiply because it combines the male and the female.

2. The number two has the power to unite and to reconcile because it is the bridge.

3. The number two has the power to magnetize and to electrify because it has a double polarity. Unlike "poles" attract to eliminate differences and form unity in diversity.

4. The number two has the power to oppose and to change because it has a double polarity. Like "poles" repel to eliminate the status quo and bring about change.

5. The number two has the power to save because it holds the Messiah in its essence.

Now, how does Barack Obama use the holy weapon of the number two to win power and dominate in the United States and the world?

1. The number two is the first and immediate production from the number one. Therefore, no other number exists between the number one and the number two. The number one does not need the participation of a third number to produce the number two—it only has to double itself. When we calculate $1 + 1 = 2$, we obtain the number two. The conclusion is that the number two is a full reflection of the number one. Also, the production of the number two depends wholly on the power and will of the number one. By virtue of this, Barack Obama, who is identified with the number two, receives full powers from God, who is identified with the number one. This is written in John 3:34–35: "The one whom God has sent speaks God's words, because God gives him the fullness of his Spirit. The Father loves his Son and has put everything in his power." Thus Barack Obama was chosen by God and marked with the number two to rule the United States and to reform the world. In fact, his first name, Barack, comes from an Arabic word that means "blessed by God" or "the anointed one."

2. Since no other whole number exists between the number one and the number two, the barriers of racial prejudice and political immaturity that stood between Barack Obama and the White House in 2008 mysteriously collapsed. In fact, they turned out to be blessings, paving his way to the presidency. Therefore, the biracial origin of Barack Obama, combined with

his diverse social experiences in Jakarta, Chicago, and New York City, help to boost his capacity as a dependable bridge between the different races in the United States and the different nations in the world. This is in line with the symbolism of the number two as the link between two points, and its power to reconcile and unite. Thus, the scriptures say in Romans 8:25–30,

> But if we hope for what we do not see, we wait for it with patience. In the same way the Spirit also comes to help us, weak as we are. For we do not know how we ought to pray; the Spirit himself pleads with God for us in groans that words cannot express. And God, who sees into our hearts, knows what the thought of the Spirit is, because the Spirit pleads with God on behalf of his people and in accordance with his will. We know that in all things God works for good with those who love him, those whom he has called according to his purpose. Those whom God had already chosen he also set apart to become like his Son, so that the Son would be the eldest brother in a large family. And so those whom God set apart, he called; and those he called, he put right with himself, and he shared his glory with them.

3. The power of opposition of the number two gave Barack Obama inspiration and courage in 2008 to reject the status quo of the White House. His campaign, therefore, stood on the platform of change. And, though that was a strange idea in the history of politics in the United States, it won the majority of votes.

4. The number two, by virtue of its power of growth and expansion, enabled Barack Obama to make

smart and spectacular political strides within a very short time. In fact, when he won the Democratic Party nomination to compete for the United States' presidency, he had served as senator for only three years—2005 to 2008.[15]

5. The magnetic and electric powers of the number two generate in Barack Obama his characteristic smartness, charm, and eloquence. No one can deny the fact that his charisma played the front role in his victorious campaigns in 2008 and 2012.

6. The power of the number two makes Barack Obama both faithful to God, who blesses him, and loyal to the American people, who elect him. This is imperative because the number two cannot exist without the number one. The emanation of the number two depends exclusively on the will and power of the number one. Thus, if the number two were to try to separate from the number one, the number two would be reabsorbed into the number one and cease to exist. When we calculate 2 - 1 = 1, we obtain the number one. Here, the number one stands for both God and the voters in the United States.

7. President Barack Obama will succeed and rule with the power of God. For, as God's grace brought him to power, he will maintain it only through faith. Thus, on January 20, 2009, when Barack Obama took the oath of office, he swore on the Bible once used by Abraham Lincoln and ended with the words, "May God help me in this task."[16] On his second inauguration on January 21, 2013, he swore on two bibles—one owned by Abraham Lincoln and the other by Martin Luther King Jr.[17]

8. President Barack Obama rules with both power and love because by virtue of the symbolism of the number two, his administration is a reflection of divine authority. In fact, he is working to present and defend a bill to regularize the status of about 11 million illegal immigrants to permit them work to earn their living and also pay taxes for the development of the United States. This is a promise that he made during his 2012 presidential campaign, and with the power of the number two he will certainly get it passed in the House of Representatives and the Senate. Thus, in John 14:10–11, it is written, "Do you not believe, Philip, that I [Jesus Christ] am in the Father and the Father is in me? The words that I have spoken to you," Jesus said to his disciples, "do not come from me. The Father, who remains in me, does his own work. Believe me when I say that I am in the Father and the Father is in me. If not, believe because of the things I do." And, in Matthew 11:27, the scriptures say, "My Father has given me all things. No one knows the Son except the Father, and no one knows the Father except the Son and those to whom the Son chooses to reveal him."

9. The linking power of the number two enables Barack Obama to reconcile and unite the different peoples of America and the different nations of the world. In doing this, he exploits his own particularity and multicultural experiences—in Jakarta, Chicago, and New York City—to consolidate the American nation and to stabilize the world. Thus, in his second inaugural speech on January 21, 2013, he reminded Americans of their unique heritage of "diversity and openness," and he invited them to "come together to seize the moment."[18]

10. The magnetic power of the number two enables Barack Obama to campaign and win the support of his political and diplomatic opponents necessary to implement his domestic and foreign policies. Thus, on January 1, 2013, he averted the dreaded fiscal cliff by successfully pushing the Senate and Congress to adopt his proposed tax increases for the top two percent of richest Americans[19.] Hence, he won another victory against the Republicans in Congress who had been very bitterly opposed to any tax increases for the rich. It was also a fulfillment of one of his key 2012 election promises.

11. The reproductive and multiplying power of the number two enables Barack Obama to stimulate the economy, create jobs, increase living standards, and consolidate the power and supremacy of the United States in the world.

12. The expansive power of the number two enables Barack Obama to consolidate the military and political power of the United States. He does it without compromising world peace and stability because his actions are guided by the Spirit of God.

13. Thus, on May 2, 2011, a secret US military mission to Pakistan hit and killed Osama bin Laden—the leader of Al Qaeda and the most-wanted enemy of the United States.[20] He had been on the run since September 11, 2001, when he hit the World Trade Center, and by killing him without war Barack Obama did what two and a half regimes in the United States had failed to do—with all the bloodshed in Kuwait, Iraq, and Afghanistan. Coincidentally, on that same day the late Pope John Paul II, who in May 1981 survived an assassination attempt by the Turkish-born terrorist

Mehmet Ali Agca, was being beatified in Rome. Now, who does not see the hand of God in the timing of these coinciding events? Do they not prove that the actions of Barack Obama are mysteriously planned and coordinated from above?

14. The magnetic and electric power of the number two have continued to boost the charisma and popularity of President Barack Obama and enabled him to win his reelection to the White House on November 6, 2012, despite his depressing economic records.

15. The revolutionary power of the number two enables Barack Obama to overcome the obstacles to change in order to apply his neopolitical ideas to save America and the world. This is demonstrated, for example, by his fight against gun abuse, climate change, and social inequalities, as was mentioned before.

16. On the international scene, the messianic power of the number two enables Barack Obama to fight against the production of dangerous arms, dictatorships, injustice, terrorism, and piracy. So, in 2009 he was awarded the Nobel Peace Prize "for his extraordinary efforts to strengthen international diplomacy and cooperation between peoples" and his "vision of and work for a world without nuclear weapons."[21] The result would be the consolidation of world peace, stability, and security, which would bring about economic, social, and human progress. Evidently, the universal mission of Barack Obama began to unfold on January 20, 2009, and the greatest is still to come.

In chapter 5, we will study the number three as a vital number of Barack Obama.

15. Edward M. Kennedy, *The American Journey of Barack Obama* (New York: Little, Brown & Co., 2008).
16. Barack Obama, *Our Enduring Spirit: President Barack Obama's First Words to America* (New York: HarperCollins, 2009).
17. BBC World News, January 21, 2013.
18. Ibid.
19. BBC World News, January 1, 2013.
20. BBC World News, May 2, 2011.
21. Nobel Foundation Awards, 2009.

Artwork 6 of 21: Equilateral Triangle. This is the symbol of perfect manifestation, perfect creation, and perfect co-existence.

CHAPTER FIVE

The Mysteries of Three

**In the beginning the Word already existed; the
Word was with God, and the Word was God.
From the very beginning the Word was with
God. Through him God made all things; not
one thing in all creation was made without
him.**

(John 1:1–3)

THE number three is numerically written as 3 and
graphically represented by a triangle. The number three is
the sum of the number two and the number one. When we
calculate 2 + 1 = 3, we obtain the number three. The number
three is also the production of a third entity by the combination
of two complementary entities. When we combine 1 + 1 = 3,
we obtain the number three. The second operation is called
the law of the triangle.[22]

The Signs of the Number Three

Before examining the symbolism of the number three and the role it played in the elections of Barack Obama, let us first determine whether the number three is one of his vital numbers. The following facts identify Barack Obama with the number three.

1. The simultaneous identity of Barack Obama with the number one and the number two, as already discussed, is enough proof of his identity with the number three. When we calculate 1 + 2 = 3, we obtain the number three.

2. Barack Obama is a unique product of two different races. His father was black, and his mother was white; but he is neither black nor white. This neutrality is not only in color but also in character. Here, the law of the triangle applies because when we combine 1 + 1 = 3, we obtain the number three.

3. Barack Obama is a unique product of two different countries in two different continents—Kenya in Africa and the United States in North America. And, although he is American by nationality, he is neither African nor American in spirit; he is a mix of both—a true citizen of the world. Here, the law of the triangle applies because when we combine 1 + 1 = 3, we obtain the number three.

4. Barack Obama was brought up in two different countries in two different continents—the United States in North America and Indonesia in Southeast Asia. So, despite the fact that he is an American, Barack Obama holds an intercontinental perspective.

Here, again, the law of the triangle operates because when we combine 1 + 1 = 3, we obtain the number three.

5. Barack Obama grew up in three different homes—the home of his mother and father, the home of his mother and stepfather, and the home of his maternal grandfather and grandmother. This is a sign of the number three.

6. The name of Barack Obama has three words—"Barack," "Hussein," and "Obama." This is a sign of the number three.

7. In the November 4, 2008, presidential election, Barack Obama won the three battleground states of Florida, Virginia, and Colorado. This is a sign of the number three.

8. On October 9, 2009, Barack Obama was awarded the Nobel Peace Prize[23] in recognition of his constructive foreign policy and peaceful engagement—especially in Iraq and the whole Middle East. The numerical reduction of this date is equal to the number three. Thus, when we calculate (10) + (9) + (2009) = 1 + 0 + 9 + 2 + 0 + 0 + 9 = 21 = 2 + 1 = 3, we obtain the number three.

9. On March 21, 2010, Barack Obama won a total of 219 against 212 votes in the House of Representatives to pass his controversial health insurance bill—Obamacare,[24] a victory that past Democrat presidents had failed to obtain since 1935. The numerical reduction of 219, the number of winning votes, is equal to the number three. When we calculate 2 + 1 + 9 = 12 = 1 + 2 = 3, we obtain the number three.

10. Furthermore, the difference between 2010 (the year in which the bill was passed) and 1935 (the year in which the campaign for the bill began) is seventy-five years. The numerical reduction of seventy-five is equal to the number three. When we calculate $7 + 5 = 12 = 1 + 2 = 3$, we obtain the number three.

11. Moreover, the numerical reduction of the date, month, and year in which the bill was passed results in the number three. First of all, considering that March is the third month of the year, we realize the number three. Second, the numerical reduction of the date of 21 is equal to the number three; when we calculate $2 + 1 = 3$, we obtain the number three. Third, the numerical reduction of the year 2010 is equal to the number three; when we calculate $2 + 0 + 1 + 0 = 3$, we obtain the number three.

These facts stand out to prove that Barack Obama is ruled by the number three and that his election and reelection as the forty-fourth president of the United States was a perfect manifestation of the law of the triangle.

The Symbolism of the Number Three

Having confirmed that Barack Obama is marked with the number three, let us now discuss the symbolism of the number three.

1. The number three symbolizes the law of the triangle, which says that for any perfect manifestation to occur there must be an interaction between two opposite and complementary principles. Thus, when we combine $1 + 1 = 3$, we obtain the number three. For example, the combination of a proton (positive principle) and an

electron (negative principle) produces electricity. And also, the combination of a sperm (male principle) and an ovum (female principle) produces a child.

2. The number three is the symbol of the Holy Trinity—Father, Son, and Holy Spirit. They all exist as one God in perfect unity. Therefore, when we combine the three, 1 + 1 + 1 = 1, we obtain the number one.

3. The number three also symbolizes the third point of this sacred triangle—the Holy Trinity. Therefore, the interaction between the Father and the Son produces the Holy Spirit. So, in John 14:16, the scriptures say, "I [Jesus Christ the Son of God] will ask the Father, and he will give you another Helper, who will stay with you forever." Also, in John 14:23, it is written, "Jesus answered him, 'Whoever loves me will obey my teaching. My Father will love him and my Father and I will come to him and live with him'"—this is the presence of the Holy Spirit. And, in John 16:7, Jesus says, "But I am telling you the truth: it is better for you that I go away, because if I do not go, the Helper will not come to you. But if I do go away, then I will send him to you." Finally, in John 7:39, it is written, "Jesus said this about the Spirit, which those who believed in him were going to receive. At that time the Spirit had not yet been given, because Jesus had not been raised to glory."

4. The number three is the symbol of perfect manifestation. Thus:

   i. In Mark 8:31, 9:30–31, 10:32–34, Jesus Christ spoke about his death three times before it happened. Also, in John 20:19–20, 26–27, 21:1, 4, 14, Jesus Christ appeared to his disciples three times between his resurrection from the dead and ascension into heaven.

ii. In Matthew 26:14–15, Jesus Christ was betrayed by Judas Iscariot for thirty pieces of silver. The numerical reduction of thirty is equal to the number three. Thus, when we calculate $3 + 0 = 3$, we obtain the number three. And, in Matthew 26:20, 26–28, Jesus Christ ate the Last Supper with twelve disciples. The numerical reduction of twelve is equal to the number three. Therefore, when we calculate $1 + 2 = 3$, we obtain the number three.

iii. In John 18:16–17, 25–27, the cock crowed when Simon Peter denied Jesus Christ three times. And in John 21:15–19, Jesus Christ said to the very Simon Peter, "Follow me!" when he accepted Jesus Christ three times.

iv. In Luke 23:44–46, Jesus Christ died on the cross three hours after his crucifixion, and in Luke 24:5–7, he rose from the dead three days after his death. These are signs of the number three.

5. As the symbol of the law of the triangle, the number three stands for both perfect creation and perfect destruction. Thus, when we combine $1 + 1 = 3$, we obtain the number three; and when we combine $(+1) + (-1) = 0$, we obtain zero. Therefore, the universe was created by the interaction of the Spirit with the Word of God. Thus, in Genesis 1:1–3 the scriptures say, "In the beginning, when God created the universe, the earth was formless and desolate. The raging ocean that covered everything was engulfed in total darkness,

and the Spirit of God was moving over the water. Then God commanded, 'Let there be light'—and light appeared." And in John 1:1–3, it is written, "In the beginning the Word already existed; the Word was with God, and the Word was God. From the very beginning the Word was with God. Through him God made all things; not one thing in all creation was made without him." On the other hand, when God was cross with human beings, he destroyed the world with his Word and a flood that lasted forty days and forty nights. This is written in Genesis 7:4, 11–12, 23:

> "Seven days from now I am going to send rain that will fall for forty days and nights, in order to destroy all the living beings that I have made." When Noah was six hundred years old, on the seventeenth day of the second month all the outlets of the vast body of water beneath the earth burst open, all the floodgates of the sky were opened, and rain fell on the earth for forty days and nights. The Lord destroyed all living beings on the earth—human beings, animals, and birds. The only ones left were Noah and those who were with him in the boat.

The Powers of the Number Three

Having examined the symbolism of the number three, we will now discuss its powers and see how Barack Obama makes use of them.

In accordance with its symbolism, the number three has the following virtues:

1. The number three has the power to perfectly create and re-create.

2. The number three has the power to perfectly act and react.

3. The number three has the power to equalize and harmonize. Thus, symbolizing the three stones on the fireplace, it has the power to uphold and stabilize.

4. The number three has the power to perfectly coexist and collaborate.

5. The number three has the power to cancel or destroy.

Now we will examine how the number three enables Barack Obama to conquer and use power.

1. The number three enabled Barack Obama in 2008 to conceive and create a solid political platform for change that won the favor of the majority of voters.

2. The number three enables Barack Obama to act effectively and react promptly. Thus, after his poor performance in the first presidential debate in 2012,[25] he bounced back in the second and third debates to overshadow his opponent, Mitt Romney.

3. The number three enables Barack Obama to gain stability and stand his ground against all adversity in the battles of the White House. Thus, in 2012 he persisted on to back his plan to increase income taxes for the richest people in the United States—and, finally, he won.

4. The number three enabled Barack Obama to create and coordinate powerful campaign teams that acted together with the rest of his supporters to obtain victory for him. In fact, in both 2008 and 2012 his

campaign teams were not only solid but also present and efficient everywhere.

5. The number three enables Barack Obama to cancel arguments and accusations made against him by his challengers and detractors. It also enables him to destroy obstacles in his way, and domestic and foreign problems coming under his ambit.

6. The number three enables Barack Obama to uphold his political platform for change as well as the prestige and supremacy of the United States.

7. The number three enabled Barack Obama in 2008 to realize both his dream for change and his ambition to rule the United States of America. Thus he won the long struggle for racial equality, begun by Martin Luther King Jr. in the 1960s, to become the first black man ever to accede to the presidency of the United States.

8. The number three, operating in the law of the triangle in 2008, realized the victory of Barack Obama in the following equations: Crises + Providence = Change, and United States + Change = Barack Obama. In fact, the September 11, 2001, terrorist attack on America, the war in Iraq, and the 2007 financial crunch and economic downturn made change a necessity for the United States. The cry for change came both from home and from abroad, invoking the divine intervention of God. This providence manifested as conditions that gave Barack Obama, the candidate of change, an advantage over the candidate of continuity—Senator John McCain. Therefore, in spite of its very painful effects, the financial crunch was a blessing to Barack Obama because it shifted

the political debate from foreign policy and war to the economy and social welfare. And there, Barack Obama had a huge advantage over his challenger and his detractors.

9. The number three, manifesting as his racial neutrality, made Barack Obama the standard of equality, justice, and stability. In fact, his multicultural background made him not only a stirring spoon in the melting pot of the United States, but also the hoped-for messiah of a world in search of tolerance, peace, and security.

10. The number three gives Barack Obama support and solidarity in his high and challenging office. It enables him to work effectively with the House of Representatives and the Senate to realize his ideas of change. In diplomacy, the number three empowers Barack Obama to create the balance of power to ensure peace and stability in the world.

11. The number three, manifesting in the law of the triangle, influences the presidency of Barack Obama in the following equations:

    i.   The United States + Barack Obama = Change. Barack Obama uses his initiative to cause change, as he declared during his 2008 campaign for the White House: "The ways of Washington must change."[26]

    ii. Barack Obama + Initiative = Change. And this change takes place not only in the economy but also in the environment and in the society.

    iii. The United States + Change = Well-Being. Thus, change interacts with the society to produce well-being by eliminating the causes of the crises that stifle the happiness of the people.

iv. The World + Barack Obama = Change. The change in foreign policy interacts with the rest of the world to produce peace and stability.

v. The World + Change = Peace. This peaceful coexistence between the United States of America and other world powers would lead to stability, security, and progress in the whole world.

Therefore, based on the merits of the number three, we can anticipate with certainty that the administration of Barack Obama will eventually eliminate the economic, political, and environmental and security problems that suffocate the United States and the world as a whole.

In chapter 6, we will discuss the number four as a vital number of Barack Obama.

---

22. Richard Taylor, *Metaphysics.* 4th ed. (Boston: Pearson, 1991).

23. Nobel Foundation Awards, 2009.

24. BBC World News, March 21, 2010.

25. CNN Television Broadcast, October 17, 2012.

26. Barack Obama, *Change We Can Believe In: Barack Obama's Plan to Renew America's Promise* (New York: Crown Publishing, 2009).

Artwork 7 of 21: Perfect Square. This is the symbol of perfection, regularity, and integrity.

CHAPTER SIX

The Mysteries of Four

For the scripture says, "I chose a valuable stone, which I am placing as the cornerstone in Zion; and whoever believes in him will never be disappointed." This stone is of great value for you that believe; but for those who do not believe, "The stone which the builders rejected as worthless turned out to be the most important of all."

(1 Peter 2:6–8)

THE number four is numerically written as 4 and geometrically represented by a perfect square.[27]

The Signs of the Number Four

The following number analyses, characteristic of Barack Obama, prove that he is truly identifiable with the number four.

1. Barack Obama was elected to the US Senate in 2004. That was the fourth year of both the third millennium and the twenty-first century. This fourth chronological position of 2004 is a sign of the number four.

2. Barack Obama was first elected US president in 2008. It was four years after his election as US senator in 2004. This is another sign of the number four.

3. Again, Barack Obama was first elected US president in 2008. It was forty years after the assassination of Martin Luther King Jr., who proclaimed that one day all Americans will be judged by their competence rather than by their color.[28] The numerical reduction of forty years is equal to the number four. Thus, when we calculate $40 = 4 + 0 = 4$, we obtain the number four.

4. The number four begins four important dates, quantities, and positions related to President Barack Obama. He was born on August 4, 1961[29] and elected on November 4, 2008, at the age of forty-seven, as the forty-fourth president of the United States. These are signs of the number four.

5. The name of Barack Obama's wife, Michelle Obama, contains thirteen letters. The numerical reduction of thirteen is equal to the number four. Thus, when we calculate $13 = 1 + 3 = 4$, we obtain the number four.

6. At school, Barack Obama had four nicknames— The One, Barry, Bama, and The Rock. The four nicknames and the rock are both signs and symbols of the number four.

7. The economic stimulus package signed by President Barack Obama on February 17, 2009, was worth $787

billion.[30] The numerical reduction of 787 billion is equal to the number four. Therefore, when we calculate $7 + 8 + 7 + 0 + 0 + 0 + 0 + 0 + 0 + 0 + 0 + 0 = 22 = 2 + 2 = 4$, we obtain the number four.

The Symbolism of the Number Four

1. The number four represents a square. The square is the symbol of perfection, regularity, and accuracy. This is the reason why a set-square is the basic instrument in building and construction. Thus, in Revelation 21:10–11, 16, the scripture says,

   > The Spirit took control of me, and the angel carried me to the top of a very high mountain. He showed me Jerusalem, the Holy City, coming down out of heaven from God and shining with the glory of God. The city shone like a precious stone, like jasper, clear as crystal. The city was perfectly square, as wide as it was long. The angel measured the city with his measuring rod: it was 2,400 kilometers long and was as wide and as high as it was long.

2. The number four symbolizes solidity and integrity. Thus, when a square is extended to a cube, there comes to being a solid with equal length, width, and height. This is written in Revelation 21:16: "The city was perfectly square, as wide as it was long. The angel measured the city with his measuring rod: it was 2,400 kilometers long and was as wide and as high as it was long."

3. The number four is the symbol of firmness, fortitude, strength, and resistance. It stands for something or someone that is solid, standard, and firmly fixed—as

a square peg in a square hole. Thus, in Ephesians 2:19–22, the scripture says,

> So then, you Gentiles are not foreigners or strangers any longer; you are now fellow-citizens with God's people and members of the family of God. You, too, are built upon the foundation laid by the apostles and prophets, the cornerstone being Christ Jesus himself. He is the one who holds the whole building together and makes it grow into a sacred temple dedicated to the Lord. In union with him you too are being built together with all the others into a place where God lives through his Spirit.

And, in 1 Peter 5:8–10, the scripture says,

> Be alert, be on the watch! Your enemy, the devil, roams round like a roaring lion, looking for someone to devour. Be firm in your faith and resist him, because you know that your fellow-believers in all the world are going through the same kind of sufferings. But after you have suffered for a little while, the God of all grace, who calls you to share his eternal glory in union with Christ, will himself perfect you and give you firmness, strength, and a sure foundation.

4. The number four symbolizes a house, which traditionally has four walls, four corners, and four pillars. Thus, in Matthew 7:24–27, it is written,

> So then, anyone who hears these words of mine and obeys them is like a wise man who built his house on rock. The rain poured down, the rivers overflowed, and the wind blew hard against that house. But it did not fall, because it was built on rock. But anyone

who hears these words of mine and does not obey them is like a foolish man who built his house on sand. The rain poured down, the rivers overflowed, the wind blew hard against that house, and it fell. And what a terrible fall that was!

5. In fact, it is in this "house" that the Holy Spirit lives to exercise the mighty power of Four, in 1 Corinthians 3:16–17, the scripture says, "Surely you know that you are God's temple and that God's Spirit lives in you! So if anyone destroys God's temple, God will destroy him. For God's temple is holy, and you yourselves are his temple." So, in Acts 2:1–4, the scripture says,

> When the day of Pentecost came, all the believers were gathered together in one place. Suddenly there was a noise from the sky which sounded like a strong wind blowing, and it filled the whole house where they were sitting. Then they saw what looked like tongues of fire which spread out and touched each person there. They were all filled with the Holy Spirit and began to talk in other languages, as the Spirit enabled them to speak.

And, in Luke 1:30–35, the scripture says,

> The angel said to her, "Don't be afraid, Mary; God has been gracious to you. You will become pregnant and give birth to a son, and you will name him Jesus. He will be great and will be called the Son of the Most High God. The Lord God will make him a king, as his ancestor David was, and he will be the king of the descendants of Jacob forever; his kingdom will never end!" Mary said to the angel, "I am a virgin. How, then, can this be?" The angel answered, "The Holy Spirit will come on you, and

God's power will rest upon you. For this reason the holy child will be called the Son of God."

Thus, the Messiah Jesus Christ was conceived by the Holy Spirit and born of the Virgin Mary, whose name also contains four letters.

6. The number four symbolizes Jesus Christ as the cornerstone and foundation of the universe. Thus, in John 1:1–5, it is written,

> In the beginning the Word already existed; the Word was with God and the Word was God. From the very beginning the Word was with God. Through him God made all things; not one thing in all creation was made without him. The Word was the source of life, and this life brought light to humanity. The light shines in the darkness, and the darkness has never put it out.

Then, in 1 Peter 2:4–8, the scriptures say,

> Come to the Lord, the living stone rejected by the people as worthless but chosen by God as valuable. Come as living stones, and let yourselves be used in building the spiritual temple, where you will serve as holy priests to offer spiritual and acceptable sacrifices to God through Jesus Christ. For the scripture says, "I chose a valuable stone, which I am placing as a cornerstone in Zion; and whoever believes in him will never be disappointed." This stone is of great value for you that believe; but for those who do not believe, "The stone which the builders rejected as worthless turned out to be the most important of all." And another scripture says, "This is the stone that will make people stumble, the rock that will

make them fall." They stumbled because they did not believe in the word; such was God's will for them.

And, in Ephesians 2:19–22, it is written,

> So then, you Gentiles are not foreigners or strangers any longer; you are now fellow-citizens with God's people and members of the family of God. You, too, are built upon the foundation laid by the apostles and prophets, the cornerstone being Christ Jesus himself. He is the one who holds the whole building together and makes it grow into a sacred temple dedicated to the Lord. In union with him you too are being built together with all the others into a place where God lives through his Spirit.

7. The number four symbolizes the four active principles in nature, which are earth, water, air, and fire. These four elements are the basis of creation, existence, and change.

8. The number four is the symbol of fullness and abundance, fertility and prosperity, as exemplified by the four rivers in the Garden of Eden. Thus in Genesis 2:10–14, the scripture says,

> A stream flowed in Eden and watered the garden; beyond Eden it divided into four rivers. The first river is the Pishon; it flows round the country of Havilah. (Pure gold is found there and also rare perfume and precious stones.) The second river is the Gihon; it flows round the country of Cush. The third river is the Tigris, which flows east of Assyria, and the fourth river is the Euphrates.

9. The number four symbolizes the cross, crucifix, or the crucifixion of Jesus Christ. The cross is a geometric representation of the number four because it has four straight arms and four right angles. It represents the suffering of Jesus Christ on the cross for the redemption of the world. Thus, in Philippians 2:8 it is written, "He [Jesus] was humble and walked the path of obedience all the way to death—his death on the cross." Then, in Hebrews 10:10, the scripture says, "Because Jesus Christ did what God wanted him to do, we are all purified from sin by the offering that he made of his own body once and for all." And, in Colossians 3:1, it is written, "You have been raised to life with Christ, so set your hearts on the things that are in heaven, where Christ sits on his throne at the right-hand side of God."

10. The number four symbolizes trials that go before uplift, enlightenment, or victory in life—it is the age of maturity. Thus, in Exodus 34:28, it is recorded that the prophet Moses received the Ten Commandments after spending forty days and nights on Mount Sinai: "Moses stayed there [on Mount Sinai] with the Lord forty days and nights, eating and drinking nothing. He wrote on the tablets the words of the covenant— the Ten Commandments." Also, after the Israelites were freed from slavery in Egypt, they wandered in the desert for forty years before arriving in Canaan, their Promised Land. This is written in Deuteronomy 29:5–6: "For forty years the Lord led you through the desert, and your clothes and sandals never wore out. You did not have bread to eat or wine or beer to drink, but the Lord provided for your needs in order to teach you that he is your God." The numerical reduction of forty is equal to the number four. Thus, when we calculate $40 = 4 + 0 = 4$, we obtain the number four.

11. Furthermore, Jesus Christ received the full power for his ministry after being tempted by the devil for forty days. This is written in Luke 4:1–2, 13–15, 16–21:

> Jesus returned from the Jordan full of the Holy Spirit and was led by the Spirit into the desert, where he was tempted by the devil for forty days. In all that time he ate nothing, so that he was hungry when it was over. When the devil finished tempting Jesus in every way, he left him for a while. Then Jesus returned to Galilee, and the power of the Holy Spirit was with him. The news about him spread throughout all that territory. He taught in the synagogues and was praised by everyone. Then Jesus went to Nazareth, where he had been brought up, and on the Sabbath he went as usual to the synagogue. He stood up to read the scriptures and was handed the book of the prophet Isaiah. He unrolled the scroll and found the place where it is written, "The Spirit of the Lord is upon me, because he has chosen me to bring good news to the poor. He has sent me to proclaim liberty to the captives and recovery of sight to the blind; to set free the oppressed and announce that the time has come when the Lord will save his people." Jesus rolled up the scroll, gave it back to the attendant, and sat down. All the people in the synagogue had their eyes fixed on him, as he said to them, "This passage of scripture has come true today, as you heard it being read."

The numerical reduction of forty is equal to the number four. Thus, when we calculate $40 = 4 + 0 = 4$, we obtain the number four. Finally, Jesus Christ ascended into heaven forty days after his death. So, it is written in Acts 1:2–3,

Before he was taken up, he gave instructions by the power of the Holy Spirit to the men he had chosen as his apostles. For forty days after his death he appeared to them many times in ways that proved beyond doubt that he was alive. They saw him, and he talked with them about the kingdom of God.

The Power of the Number Four

Having examined the symbolism of the number four, we will go on to discuss how it enables Barack Obama to conquer and exercise power.

1. The number four enables Barack Obama to receive knowledge, wisdom, authority, and the grace of God to conquer and use political power. Therefore, in the 2008 campaign he received the benefit of the unforeseen financial crunch and economic downturn to advance his cause for change. Also, in 2012 he took advantage of Hurricane Sandy and reacted promptly and efficiently to again express his concern for the American people.

2. The number four gave Barack Obama the conviction, resolve, and audacity to stand for the presidency of the United States, for the first time, in 2008.

3. The number four enables Barack Obama to stand firm and strong on his platform for change and to concretely defend his political, economic, and social agenda.

4. The number four enabled Barack Obama to conceive and execute strong political campaigns in 2008 and 2012—and to effectively apply them to obtain victory.

5. The number four enabled Barack Obama to stand against adversity—accusations, calumny, and intimidation—and to overcome fear, in spite of attempts to assassinate him during the 2008 presidential campaign.[31]

6. The number four makes Barack Obama steadfast, steady, receptive, tolerant, and calm in the face of disagreement, conflict, and adversity.

7. The number four enables Barack Obama to uphold the American Constitution, founded on liberty, justice, and equality. He transforms these principles into concrete realities in the United States, even in the midst of controversy. This is seen, for example, in his strong support for homosexuals and gay rights. In his capacity as president of the United States, Barack Obama is also the rock and foundation of a new world order of justice, peace, and security.

8. The number four enables Barack Obama to carry the cross of the United States and the whole world. This cross consists of the financial crunch, economic downturn, insecurity, gun abuse, terrorism, diplomatic friction, and climate change. Consequently, he makes great sacrifices necessary to solve these burning issues. However, these sacrifices are not his body and blood, as was the sacrifice that Jesus Christ made to save the world. For only the blood of Jesus could save the world, and it was shed once and for all. So in Hebrews 10:10, 18, the scriptures say, "Because Jesus Christ did what God wanted him to do, we are all purified from sin by the offering that he made of his own body once and for all. So when these have been forgiven, an offering to take away sins is no longer needed." The sacrifices of President Barack Obama are that he

has to make very delicate decisions and important compromises, which are sometimes out of "the ways of Washington." When he succeeds he is a double hero, and when he fails he bears the blame.

9. The number four gives Barack Obama the strength, soundness, and determination to work hard in the execution of his functions.

10. The number four gives Barack Obama the courage, bravery, and authority needed to prescribe unprecedented solutions to the unprecedented problems facing the United States and the whole world today.

11. The number four enables Barack Obama to withstand adversity and overcome the obstacles in his high office. According to the symbolism of the number four, anything that is completely solid and perfectly square can be firmly fixed and made to endure adversity and to withstand all challenges. In practice, therefore, Barack Obama is squarely facing all the challenges that confront him now as president of the United States. From the number four, he draws the courage, strength, and firmness needed to make changes for the regeneration of the United States and the progress of the world.

12. The number four enables Barack Obama to be tough and resolute in his confrontation and negotiation with other political forces in the United States and in the world. In addition to this, he possesses the power of the Word—his oratory. In fact, on January 1, 2013, he successfully pushed both the House of Representatives and the Senate to vote for his planned tax increases on the richest Americans. And by this he averted the

much-dreaded fiscal cliff and scored a spectacular goal even before the beginning of his second term in the White House.

13. The number four enables Barack Obama to make the United States more solid and perfect, and to regularize her financial system for the emergence of a stronger economy. The presidency of Barack Obama, empowered by the number four, is leading America to a new takeoff that will permit her to reinvent her dream and reconfirm her superiority and supremacy in the world. So in his second inaugural speech on January 21, 2013, Barack Obama pledged to maintain the status of the United States as the world's superpower, but without compromising world peace and stability.

14. The number four enables Barack Obama to bring peace and stability to the world. Despite the recurring diplomatic frictions and military tensions around the world, the growing understanding between the United States and China and the efforts of the Obama administration for peace, especially in the Middle East and the Korean peninsula, are bearing good fruits. No doubt, on January 21, 2013, President Barack Obama announced the ending of a decade of war.[32]

15. The number four will enable Barack Obama to endure, to persist, to overcome, and to stay in office. Surely, the power of the number four will defy all obstacles and give the Obama administration strength, endurance, and efficiency in his eight years of rule.

In chapter 7, we will discuss the number five as a vital number of Barack Obama.

27. A perfect square has all four sides equal in length and each angle equal to 90 degrees, or right angles.
28. "I Have a Dream," speech delivered by Martin Luther King Jr., Washington, DC, August 28, 1963.
29. www.barack-obama-bio.com.
30. CNN News, February 17, 2009.
31. ABC News, October 27, 2008.
32. CNN News (President Barack Obama's inauguration speech), January 21, 2013.

Artwork 8 of 21: Pentagram. This is the symbol of
enlightenment, empowerment, and victory.

CHAPTER SEVEN

The Mysteries of Five

But when the Holy Spirit comes upon you, you will be filled with power, and you will be witnesses for me in Jerusalem, in all Judea and Samaria, and to the ends of the earth.

(Acts 1:8)

THE number five is numerically written as 5. It is geometrically represented by the pentagon (a plane figure with five sides and five angles) and the pentagram (a star with five branches).

The Signs of the Number Five

We will begin by examining the association between Barack Obama and the number five. In the following numerical analyses, we will find evidence to establish his identity with the number five.

1. His last name, Obama, contains five letters. This is a sign of the number five.

2. On November 4, 2008, Barack Obama received a total of 69,445,229 popular votes[33] to win the presidential ballot. The numerical reduction of this figure is equal to the number five. Thus, when we calculate 69,445,229 = 6 + 9 + 4 + 4 + 5 + 2 + 2 + 9 = 41 = 4 + 1 = 5, we obtain the number five.

3. On November 4, 2008, Barack Obama obtained a total 365 electoral votes[34] to win the presidential election. The numerical reduction of 365 is equal to the number five. Thus, when we calculate 365 = 3 + 6 + 5 = 14 = 1 + 4 = 5, we obtain the number five.

4. President Barack Obama was born in Hawaii, which is the fiftieth state of the United States. The numerical reduction of fifty is equal to the number five. Thus, when we calculate 50 = 5 + 0 = 5, we obtain the number five.

5. Barack Obama was the fourteenth Democrat to be elected president of the United States. The numerical reduction of fourteen is equal to the number five. Thus, the calculation of 14 = 1 + 4 = 5 yields the number five.

6. Barack Obama became a US senator in 2005, which was the fifth year of both the third millennium and the twenty-first century. This is a sign of the number five.

7. President Barack Obama was inaugurated for the first time on January 20, 2009. The numerical reduction of this date is equal to the number five. Thus, the

calculation of (01) + (20) + (2009) = 0 + 1 + 2 + 0 + 2 + 0 + 0 + 9 = 14 = 1 + 4 = 5 yields the number five.

Having made certain that Barack Obama is a phenomenon animated by the number five, we will move forward to examine the symbolism of this number.

The Symbolism of the Number Five

1. The number five symbolizes the incarnation of God in man, giving birth to the Lord Jesus Christ. Thus, in John 1:14, the scripture says, "The Word became a human being and, full of grace and truth, lived among us. We saw his glory, the glory which he received as the Father's only Son." The number five is, therefore, the sum of the number four and the number one. Thus, the calculation of 4 + 1 = 5 yields the number five.

2. The number five is the symbol of the pentagon—a plane figure with five straight sides and five angles. This pentagon is also a symbol of power. Hence, the headquarters of the US Department of Defense in Washington, DC, called the Pentagon, is actually shaped like a regular pentagon.

3. The number five is the symbol of the pentagram—a star with five branches. The pentagram is a geometric figure that contains five exterior points, five identical straight lines, five identical triangles, and five intersections, all enclosing a pentagon in the center. The natural position of the pentagon inside the pentagram has a profound spiritual and material significance. It evokes and supports the idea that material power (the pentagon) must be contained by

spiritual power (the pentagram) in order to complete the plan of God. In other words, for power to serve humanity it must be held and exercised by an inspired and caring ruler. Therefore, the sum of the pentagram and the pentagon, which are both symbolized by the number five, is equal to the number one—the Almighty God. Thus, the calculation of $5 + 5 = 10 = 1 + 0 = 1$ yields the number one.

4. The number five is the symbol of Pentecost—the coming of the Holy Spirit on the apostles of Jesus Christ. The prefix "penta" in the word "Pentecost" means "five" or "having five." Thus, in Acts 2:1–4, it is written, "When the day of Pentecost came, all the believers were gathered together in one place. Suddenly there was a noise from the sky which sounded like a strong wind blowing, and it filled the whole house where they were sitting. Then they saw what looked like tongues of fire which spread out and touched each person there. They were all filled with the Holy Spirit and began to talk in other languages, as the Spirit enabled them to speak."

5. The number five symbolizes the pentagonal dimension of the human being, which includes body, mind, heart, spirit, and soul.

6. The number five is the symbol of the breath of life or divine breath by which God animated man formed from the dust of the earth. In Genesis 2:7, it is written, "Then the Lord God took some soil from the ground and formed a man out of it; he breathed life-giving breath into his nostrils and the man began to live." Therefore, man came into being only when the essence of the number one, the Spirit of God, combined with the substance of the number four, the soil of the earth.

The number five, in fact, symbolizes power, conquest, and dominion. It is the essence of life, the coming of the Holy Spirit upon man to give him direction, wisdom, and power to conquer and dominate the world. Thus, in John 6:63, the scripture says, "What gives life is God's Spirit; human power is of no use at all. The words I [Jesus Christ] have spoken to you bring God's life-giving Spirit." Then in John 16:13–15, it continues: "When, however, the Spirit comes, who reveals the truth about God; he will lead you into all the truth. He will not speak on his own authority, but he will speak of what he hears, and will tell you of things to come. He will give me glory, because he will take what I say and tell it to you. All that my father has is mine; that is why I said that the Spirit will take what I give him and tell it to you." And in Acts 1:8, the scripture says, "But when the Holy Spirit comes upon you, you will be filled with power, and you will be witnesses for me in Jerusalem, in all Judea and Samaria, and to the ends of the earth."

7. The number five is the symbol of light and transformation. The symbolism of the number five is revealed in the transfigurations of Moses and Jesus. In Exodus 34:29–30, the scripture says, "When Moses went down from Mount Sinai carrying the Ten Commandments, his face was shining because he had been speaking with the Lord; but he did not know it. Aaron and all the people looked at Moses and saw that his face was shining, and they were afraid to go near him." And in Luke 9:28–29, it is written, "About a week after he had said these things, Jesus took Peter, John, and James with him and went up a hill to pray. While he was praying, his face changed its appearance, and his clothes became dazzling white."

8. The number five symbolizes the head of a person, without which he or she cannot think; the five senses, without which he or she cannot perceive the environment; and the thumb, without which he or she cannot hold something.

9. The number five symbolizes the peak of a mountain and the roof of a house.

10. The number five is the symbol of excellence, fulfillment, and glory—the radiance of a star.

In the next section we will discuss the powers of the number five.

The Powers of the Number Five

By virtue of its symbolism, the number five has the following merits:

1. The number five has the power to revive and to restore.

2. The number five has the power to transform and to change.

3. The number five has the power to reveal and to shine.

4. The number five has the power to overcome, conquer, and dominate.

5. The number five has the power to excel and to achieve.

Let us now discuss how Barack Obama makes use of the powers symbolized by the number five to conquer and rule.

1. The number five revealed the merits of Barack Obama, radiated his magnetism, and elevated him from an ordinary black man to an eminent statesman and the most popular politician of the twenty-first century. It gave him excellence, enlightenment, and spiritual power, which boosted his performance and enabled him to win the presidency of the United States.

2. The number five gives President Barack Obama excellence and competency in the performance of his functions.

3. The number five gives Barack Obama the power to fight, overpower, and dominate his opponents in the domestic and foreign politics of the United States.

4. The number five gives Barack Obama the power to contain, fight, and overcome the record challenges facing the United States and the world today. They include the financial crunch and economic downturn, terrorism and insecurity, unemployment and poverty, arms and conflicts, and pollution and climate change.

5. The number five enables Barack Obama to exercise his authority and power to effectively fight dangerous arms, terrorism, and piracy. Thus, on May 2, 2011, he ordered a squad of the American special forces to track down and kill Osama bin Laden[35]—the man who masterminded the September 11, 2001, terrorist attacks on the United States.

6. The number five enables Barack Obama to consolidate and expand the power of the United States in the world. In his diplomatic engagements with Russia, China, and the emerging world powers, he fights to maintain the balance of political, economic, scientific,

cultural, and military power in favor of the supremacy of the United States. Now, in his second term of office, he is still developing strategies and building diplomatic alliances to frustrate the efforts of Iran and North Korea to develop nuclear weapons. Besides, on April 2, 2013, President Barack Obama announced the allocation of $100 million to carry out research in neurotechnology in order to discover, according to him, "the enormous mystery waiting to be unlocked in the human brain."

7. Finally, the union of the pentagram and the pentagon enables Barack Obama to master power in Washington and to use it to build rather than destroy. We explained at the beginning of this chapter that a pentagram is a regular plane figure with five equal and straight sides, five equidistant points, and five identical triangles, all enclosing an irregular pentagon in the center. We also demonstrated that the sum of the pentagram and its pentagon is equal to the number one Thus, the calculation of $5 + 5 = 10 = 1 + 0 = 1$ yields the number one—the symbol of God. The pentagram represents Barack Obama—the man who is empowered by God. On the other hand, the pentagon stands for the United States of America, which is the superpower of the world, and whose military headquarters is the Pentagon in Washington, DC. This geometric figure shows that the pentagram is regular because its sides and angles are alike; and the pentagon is irregular because its sides and angles are not alike. There, as the irregular pentagon is contained within the regular pentagram, so also power in Washington is subject to the integrity of Barack Obama. Under his administration, the power of America does not decline or blow up; it is safe to serve the very ideals

that the man stands for—liberty, equality, justice, peace, security, and progress.

8.   Surely, if the world has to change, the assignment of power, too, must change. If power was used in the past to conquer and oppress, today it should be used to liberate and serve. Thanks to Barack Obama, power will no longer be used to dictate but to emancipate— and the main battlefields are shifting away from expansionism and territorial claims to terrorism, drug trafficking, and piracy. Thus, the development of weapons of mass destruction will give way to humanitarian assistance, the preservation of the environment, and the promotion of good government. In fact, the challenges of the twenty-first century are many and diverse, and in the face of these, power can no longer be misused but must be appropriately used for the well-being of humanity. This will fulfill the scriptures written in Micah 4:1–4:

> In days to come the mountain where the temple stands will be the highest one of all, towering above all the hills. Many nations will come streaming to it, and their people will say, "Let us go up the hill of the Lord to the temple of Israel's God. He will teach us what he wants us to do; we will walk in the paths he has chosen. For the Lord's teaching comes from Jerusalem; from Zion he speaks to his people." He will settle disputes among the nations, among the great powers near and far. They will hammer their swords into ploughs and their spears into pruning knives. Nations will never again go to war, never prepare for battle again. Everyone will live in peace among his own vineyards and fig trees, and no one will make him afraid. The Lord Almighty has promised this.

In chapter 8, we will examine the number eight as a vital number of Barack Obama.

---

33. CNN News, November 5, 2008.

34. Ibid.

35. BBC World News, May 2, 2011.

Artwork 9 of 21: Perfect Square in Perfect Square. This is the symbol of firmness, harmony, and stability.

CHAPTER EIGHT

The Mysteries of Eight

> He will settle disputes among great nations.
> They will hammer their swords into ploughs
> and their spears into pruning knives. Nations
> will never again go to war, never prepare for
> battle again. He will judge the poor fairly
> and defend the rights of the helpless. At his
> command the people will be punished, and
> evil persons will die. He will rule his people
> with justice and integrity. Wolves and sheep
> will live together in peace, and leopards will
> lie down with young goats. Calves and lion
> cubs will feed together, and little children will
> take care of them.
>
> (Isaiah 1:4; 11:4–6)

THE number eight is numerically written as 8, and geometrically represented by the octagon—a plane figure with eight sides and eight angles.

The Signs of the Number Eight

Let us begin by finding the relationship between Barack Obama and the number eight. This will enable us to prove that the number eight is one of his vital numbers.

1. In chapters 4 and 6 we concluded that the number two and the number four are vital numbers of Barack Obama. The fact that he has identities with both the number two and the number four also gives him the identity of the number eight. This is because the number eight is the product of the number two and the number four. Thus, when we calculate 4 x 2 = 8, we obtain the number eight.

2. Barack Obama was born on August 4, 1961. August is the eighth month of the year—and this is a sign of the number eight. Moreover, the numerical reduction of 1961 is equal to the number eight. Thus, when we calculate 1961 = 1 + 9 + 6 + 1 = 17 = 1 + 7 = 8, we obtain the number eight.

3. Barack Obama was first elected in 2008 as the forty-fourth president of the United States. The numerical reduction of forty-four is equal to the number eight. Thus, when we calculate 44 = 4 + 4 = 8, we obtain the number eight.

4. Barack Obama was first elected president in 2008, which was the eighth year of the first decade of both the third millennium and the twenty-first century. The chronological position of 2008 as the eighth year is a sign of the number eight.

5. President Barack Obama was inaugurated in 2009, 233 years after the American Declaration of Independence in 1776. The numerical reduction of 233 years is equal to the number eight. Thus, when we calculate 233 = 2 + 3 + 3 = 8, we obtain the number eight.

6. As a US presidential candidate, Barack Obama addressed a crowd of 215,000 people on July 24, 2008, at Berlin in Germany.[36] The numerical reduction of 215,000 is equal to the number eight. Thus, when we calculate 215,000 = 2 + 1 + 5 + 0 + 0 + 0 = 8, we obtain the number eight.

7. When Barack Obama was elected president in 2008, his wife, Michelle, was forty-four years old. The numerical reduction of forty-four is equal to the number eight. Thus, when we calculate 44 = 4 + 4 = 8, we obtain the number eight.

8. When President Barack Obama was being sworn in for the first time on January 20, 2009, the atmospheric temperature in Washington, DC, was seventeen degrees centigrade.[37] The numerical reduction of seventeen is equal to the number eight. Thus, when we calculate 17 = 1 + 7 = 8, we obtain the number eight.

9. The public swearing-in of President Barack Obama to his second term of office took place at Capitol Hill on January 21, 2012, in the presence of 800,000 people.[38] The numerical reduction of 800,000 is equal to the number eight. Thus, when we calculate 8 + 0 + 0 + 0 + 0 = 8, we obtain the number eight.

In the following section we will discuss the symbolism of the number eight.

The Symbolism of the Number Eight

1. The number eight is geometrically represented by the octagon—a plane figure with eight equal sides and eight equal angles. The octagon symbolizes a committed person in an office, because every angle in a regular octagon is obtuse; that is, less than 180 degrees.

2. Also, the number eight is geometrically represented by a right-angle cross within a square. It is the union between material and spiritual power that qualifies man as an image of God. This symbolizes a right person in an office—because the right-angle cross stands for regularity, strength, and competence. Thus, in Genesis 1:26, 5:1, the scripture says, "Then God said, 'And now we will make human beings; they will be like us and resemble us. They will have power over the fish, the birds, and all animals, domestic and wild, large and small.' This is the list of the descendants of Adam. When God created human beings he made them like himself."

3. Equally, the number eight is geometrically represented by a square within a square. This symbolizes stability and peace, resulting from tolerance and accommodation of others. The reason for this is that the number eight is a double square. Thus, when we calculate 4 x 2 = 8, we obtain the number eight. Consequently, the number eight represents the stability that results from an agreement between two things that are put together for any purpose.

4. The number eight is also the symbol of serenity, tolerance, and harmony because it remains the same

and valid, whether you place it upright or upside down. The number eight, therefore, symbolizes that which is both active and stable. By virtue of this, it has the power not only to accomplish but also to harmonize things and situations.

5. The number eight is the symbol of reconciliation. This is because it maintains both the essence of the number two and the substance of the number four in perfect harmony. The number eight is the product of the number four and the number two. Thus, when we calculate $4 \times 2 = 8$, we obtain the number eight. Also, the number eight is the cube of the number two. Thus, when we calculate $2^3 = 2 \times 2 \times 2 = 8$, we obtain the number eight. Therefore, because the number eight draws its essence from the number two and its substance from the number four, it represents the one who has the power to reconcile humanity with God, and the body with the Spirit. And by extension, the number eight represents the one who reconciles humanity with the society, the society with the environment, and nations of the world with the world as one.

6. The number eight is the symbol of miracles and transformation because it is the second power of the number four. As we discussed earlier, the number four stands for material perfection, while the number two stands for the incarnation of God in man. Also, the power of three that converts the number two into the number eight stands for the Holy Spirit through whom God works miracles. The number eight as the symbol of transformation is well rooted in the Bible. In fact, the Transfiguration of Jesus Christ happened eight days after he told his disciples to carry their cross and follow him. And thus, in Luke 9:23, 28–29,

the scripture says, "And he said to them all, 'Anyone who wants to come with me must forget self, take up their cross every day, and follow me.' About a week (eight days) after he had said these things, Jesus took Peter, John, and James with him and went up a hill to pray. While he was praying, his face changed its appearance, and his clothes became dazzling white." Therefore, the problems encountered by the number four are transformed by the number eight through the number two and the number three. Thus, when we calculate 4 x 2 = 8, we obtain the number eight. And when we calculate 2^3 = 2 x 2 x 2 = 8, we obtain the number eight. This is the reason why the number eight holds not only the power of harmony but also the power of victory.

In the next section we will examine the ways in which Barack Obama benefits from powers that are symbolically represented by the number eight.

The Powers of the Number Eight

1. In practice, the number eight enabled Barack Obama to perform the miracle of transformation from an unknown, through merit, to victory and fame. The conjunction of personal qualities with environmental and circumstantial factors produced a miracle, which was the election in 2008 and reelection in 2012 of Barack Obama as the first-ever African American president.

2. The number eight gave Barack Obama the harmony, stability, and serenity necessary to face the challenges, adversity, and dangers that confronted him during the 2008 campaign for the White House. Evidently,

it was thanks to harmony and stability that Barack Obama had the great strength required to stand his ground against his political challengers—Senator John McCain in 2008 and former Governor Mitt Romney in 2012. President Barack Obama continues to use his profound serenity to counter and overcome the enormous challenges that are inherent in his office.

3. The number eight enables Barack Obama to harmonize his political, economic, and social plans with the circumstances and exigencies of the time. This happened in 2008, and in fact, his political slogan—"Change We Need, Change We Can Believe In"[39]—really matched the conditions of the time. There were, among other problems, the financial crunch, economic downturn, unemployment, housing crisis, gun abuse, insecurity, and diplomatic hostilities. And all these provoked a cry for change. The number eight continually enables President Barack Obama to match his actions with his political platform, his promises, and the aspirations of the American people.

4. The number eight empowered Barack Obama to be the "square peg in the square hole" of the United States. He stood in 2008 as the most competent candidate to save the American financial system, reverse the economic downturn, redress the Social Security system, and redeem the power and the prestige of the United States. He was considered to be a square peg in a square hole because the social, economic, and political conditions at that time squared up with his principles and qualities. In other words, there was a strong agreement between his ideology and the reality of the time. Like Jesus Christ, Barack Obama remains the same today as he was in 2008, because no one, yet, has proposed better solutions to the problems of the

United States and those of the world. The proof is that on November 6, 2012, he was reelected with the same enthusiasm for a second term in the White House.

5. The number eight enables President Barack Obama to integrate the different races and classes of people in the United States into a solid and powerful nation. It also enables him to concert with other nations in deliberations on international affairs in order to act together for peace and security in the world. Therefore, during his second inauguration, on January 21, 2013, he reminded Americans of their unique heritage of "diversity and openness" and challenged them to "come together to seize the moment."[40]

6. The number eight enabled President Barack Obama to win a second term in office. Thus, he will rule the United States for a duration of eight years. This possibility was inevitable because of his power identities of the three numbers that govern the presidency of the United States. They are the number four, because the presidential term lasts for four years; the number two, because the presidential terms are limited to a maximum of two; and the number eight, because two presidential terms last for eight years. Of course, in chapters 4, 6, and 8 we have demonstrated and proved that the numbers two, four, and eight are vital numbers of Barack Obama.

7. Finally, the number eight makes the administration of President Barack Obama harmonious and stable. In fact, despite all the obstacles and challenges that are facing him in the White House, his presidency is successful and fruitful. It will end with the realization of complete change and fulfillment of his promises to the American people. In his inaugural speech on

January 20, 2009, Barack Obama declared that it was time to start the work of "remaking America," that the economy needed "bold, fast steps," and that the task will not be completed in a single term of office.[41] In fact, he won a second term of office on November 6, 2012, and was, consequently, sworn in on January 21, 2013. The future is bright, and time will tell.

In chapter 9, we will discuss the plague of blood as a sacred weapon of Barack Obama.

36. *New York Times*, July 24, 2008.

37. CNN News, January 20, 2009.

38. BBC News, January 21, 2013.

39. Barack Obama, *Change We Can Believe In: Barack Obama's Plan to Renew America's Promise* (New York: Crown Publishing, 2009).

40. CNN News, January 21, 2013.

41. Barack Obama, *Our Enduring Spirit: President Barack Obama's First Words to America* (New York: HarperCollins, 2009).

Artwork 10 of 21: Positive and Negative Signs in Circle. This is the symbol of life in the blood cells of the body.

CHAPTER NINE

The Plague of Blood

Then Moses and Aaron did as the Lord commanded. In the presence of the king and his officers, Aaron raised his stick and struck the surface of the river, and all the water in it was turned into blood. The fish in the water died, and it smelt so bad that the Egyptians could not drink from it. There was blood everywhere in Egypt.

(Exodus 7:20–21)

THE last chapter was about the number eight as a vital number of Barack Obama. In this chapter we will discuss the plague of blood, which represents the faith of Barack Obama.

Background

The power of faith rules the initiatives and activities of people because it is the basis of every engagement in life.

Faith appeals to providence, faith fuels hope, and faith upholds determination, patience, and perseverance. Therefore, no one can do something without trust in his or her own ability, and nobody can receive a blessing without faith in God. This is what the scripture says in Mark 11:22–24:

> Jesus answered them, "Have faith in God. I assure you that whoever tells this hill to get up and throw itself into the sea and does not doubt in his heart, but believes that what he says will happen, it will be done for him. For this reason I tell you: when you pray and ask for something, believe that you have received it, and you will be given whatever you ask for."

Hence, those who perform miracles do no more than screw their faith to the impact point where dream is turned to reality.

Faith and the blood of Jesus are fatal weapons against the devil—the common enemy of God and man. In Ephesians 6:16, the scriptures say, "At all times carry faith as a shield; for with it you will be able to put out all the burning arrows shot by the evil one." And in Revelation 12:11, it is written, "Our brothers and sisters won the victory over him by the blood of the Lamb and by the truth which they proclaimed; and they were willing to give up their lives and die." Faith sealed the contract between Barack Obama and the people of the United States ("Yes, We Can")[42] as the blood of Jesus Christ sealed the covenant between God and the people of Israel. Thus, in Mark 14:24, the scriptures say, "Jesus said, This is my blood which is poured out for many, my blood which seals God's covenant."

The Plague of Blood

In Exodus 7:5–7, the scripture says, "The Egyptians will then know that I am the Lord, when I raise my hand against them and bring the Israelites out of their country. Moses and Aaron did what the Lord commanded. At the time when they spoke to the king, Moses was eighty years old, and Aaron was eighty-three." This scripture reveals a strong similarity between the pair Moses and Aaron, and the couple Barack and Michelle Obama. When Barack Obama ran for president in 2008, he was forty-seven years old, and Aaron was eighty-three years old when God commanded him and Moses to lead the Israelites out of Egypt. The numerical reduction of forty-seven is equal to the number two, and the numerical reduction of eighty-three is also equal to the number two. Thus, when we calculate $47 = 4 + 7 = 11 = 1 + 1 = 2$, we obtain the number two; and when we calculate $83 = 8 + 3 = 11 = 1 + 1 = 2$, we also obtain the number two.

Similarly, in 2008, the wife of Barack Obama, Michelle, was forty-four years old, and Moses was eighty years old when God commanded him and Aaron to lead the Israelites out of Egypt. The numerical reduction of forty-four is equal to the number eight, and the numerical reduction of eighty is also equal to the number eight. Thus, when we calculate $44 = 4 + 4 = 8$, we obtain the number eight; and when we calculate $80 = 8 + 0 = 8$, we also obtain the number eight. Here, therefore, Michelle stands for Moses and Barack stands for Aaron.

Finally, in Exodus 7:20–21, the scriptures say, "Then Moses and Aaron did as the Lord commanded. In the presence of the king and his officers, Aaron raised his stick and struck the surface of the river, and all the water in it was turned into blood. The fish in the water died, and it smelt so bad that the Egyptians could not drink from it. There was blood everywhere in Egypt." Here, Egypt personifies the challengers and enemies of Barack Obama as well as the problems of the United States and the world. On the other hand, Israel represents the people of America and the citizens of the world.

In the next section we will establish the evidence of faith in Barack Obama.

The Signs of Faith

The faith of Barack Obama is both strong and remarkable. In fact, he believes in himself and his ability to achieve, he believes in America and her capacity to change, and he believes in God and his power of grace.

1. Evidently, the fact that Barack Obama dared to compete for the presidency of the United States of America in 2008, in spite of the racial prejudice that weighed against him at that time, was a spectacular show of faith in his ability, faith in change, and faith in God.

2. Besides, his power of faith is clearly portrayed in his speeches. For example, when Barack Obama declares that "the ways of Washington must change," "America remains a place where everything is possible," "together, we can," "with God we will succeed," and "may God bless America,"[43] everyone can see that his faith is strong and firm.

The Sources of Faith

Having examined the evidence of faith in Barack Obama, we will now discuss how he acquired this very powerful weapon. Like many of his qualities, the faith of Barack Obama is partly inborn and partly acquired through education, training, and experience. From the spiritual sphere, Barack Obama benefits from the combined powers of the numbers one, two, and four. (This has already been discussed in chapters 3, 4, and 6.)

1. The number one, symbolizing the Creator, the beginning, and independence, gives him the powers

of creativity, supremacy, and autonomy. And these are the elements that make him believe in his ability to achieve.

2. The number two, as a faithful projection of the number one, makes Barack Obama believe strongly in God, the Creator. This is because, as we already know, $2 = 1 + 1$ and $2 - 1 = 1$. This means that the number two is a projection of the number one, and the number two cannot exist without the number one. In other words, the number two (the Son) depends fully on the number one (the Father), from whom he receives power and authority. So the number one is fully present and active in the number two. Thus, in John 3:34–35, it is written, "The one whom God has sent speaks God's words, because God gives him the fullness of his Spirit. The Father loves his Son and has put everything in his power." Then, in John 14:10–11, it is written, "'Do you not believe, Philip, that I am in the Father and the Father is in me? The words that I have spoken to you,' Jesus said to his disciples, 'do not come from me. The Father, who remains in me, does his own work. Believe me when I say that I am in the Father and the Father is in me. If not, believe because of the things I do.'" And, in John 16:15, the scripture says, "All that my Father has is mine; that is why I said that the Spirit will take what I give him and tell it to you."

3. The number four, symbolizing strength, firmness, and fitness, enhances the capabilities, determination, and fortitude of Barack Obama. This symbolism has a double effect: the first fixes his faith in God, making it firm and strong; and the second boosts his confidence, and hence his ability to act effectively.

4. On the human plane, the faith of Barack Obama comes from his excellence. In fact, he is able to do great things and does everything in a big way. His excellence, in turn, is enhanced by his nature, upbringing, education, training, and practice.

5. The past achievements of Barack Obama—academics, politics, writing, social work, and oratory—have done much to deepen and fortify his faith, faith in God, faith in himself, and faith in America.

In the following section we will discuss how Barack Obama uses the sacred weapon of faith to conquer and exercise power in the White House.

The Power of Faith

1. Faith sustains hope and fans the determination to achieve. Barack Obama has faith in himself, faith in the United States, and faith in God, which enhance both his confidence and his determination to succeed—and, in fact, through faith he wins. Thus, in his second inaugural speech delivered at Capitol Hill on January 21, 2013, President Barack Obama said, amongst other things, that "America's possibilities are limitless" and emanate from its "diversity and openness."

2. Furthermore, according to the law of spiritual magnetism, which says that like beings attract and unlike beings repel, Barack Obama's faith in America also attracts America's faith in Barack Obama. Thus, amidst the most challenging circumstances, Barack Obama was elected in 2008 and reelected in 2012

as the first-ever African American president of the United States.

3. Following the law of equal and opposite reaction (Isaac Newton—to every action there is an equal and opposite reaction), Barack Obama's action of having faith in God brings him an equal reaction of divine favor in decisive times. In fact, the incident of the financial crunch in 2008 shifted the electoral debate from foreign policy and wars to the economy and social security. As a consequence, his archrival, Senator John McCain, lost his key ground and gave Barack Obama his stronghold. Certainly, neither John McCain nor Barack Obama had anticipated the financial crunch, although the latter was campaigning for change. It came by chance and repositioned the political game. We can conclude, therefore, that the financial crunch in 2008 was more of a blessing than a misfortune to the United States of America because it gave her the opportunity to make a bet on change by electing Barack Obama. And thus the scriptures say in Mark 11:22–23, "Jesus answered them, 'Have faith in God. I assure you that whoever tells this hill to get up and throw itself in the sea and does not doubt in his heart, but believes that what he says will happen, it will be done for him.'"

4. In practice, Barack Obama's triple faith—faith in God, faith in America, and faith in himself—will continue to enhance his determination and courage to bring about change and face the challenges of the time. Definitely, his will and determination will meet with the loyalty and collaboration of the American people, given the popularity that elected him in 2008 and maintained him in power in 2012.

In chapter 10, we will look at the plague of frogs as a sacred weapon of Barack Obama.

---

42. Barack Obama, *Our Enduring Spirit: President Barack Obama's First Words to America* (New York: HarperCollins, 2009).

43. Ibid.

Artwork 11 of 21: Frog. This is a small animal with smooth skin that lives both on land and in water.

CHAPTER TEN

The Plague of Frogs

The Nile will be so full of frogs that they will
leave it and go into your palace, your bedroom,
your bed, the houses of your officials and your
people, and even into your ovens and baking
pans. They will jump up on you, your people,
and your officials. The Lord said to Moses,
"Tell Aaron to hold out his stick over the
rivers, the canals, and the pools, and make
frogs come up and cover the land of Egypt." So
Aaron held it out over all the water, and frogs
came out and covered the land.

(Exodus 8:3–6)

THE previous chapter discussed the plague of blood as the
faith of Barack Obama. This chapter is about the plague[44]
of frogs, which symbolizes the courage of President Barack
Obama. For the audacity of Barack Obama is as impressive as
his historic victories in 2008 and 2012.

Background

Courage is the first step to accomplishment because nothing can be done without the risk of failure; and more often than not, failure is associated with danger. In fact, every enterprise has a risk, no matter the safety of the circumstance and the expertise of the actor. To act, therefore, is to expect either success or failure, and to be ready to accept the consequences of either one. In fact, the power of courage has taken as many people to the top as it has taken to the depths.

The Plague of Frogs

For a frog to leap out of a river and go into a palace is a great feat of courage—yet unrecorded in history. But Barack Obama did leap wonderfully from the archipelagoes of Hawaii into the glory of the White House, when he was still unknown. The frogs represent Barack Obama and all those who, through courage, spring from their low births to positions of power and fame. Thus in Exodus 8:1–6, the scriptures say,

> Then the Lord said to Moses, "Go to the king and tell him that the Lord says, 'Let my people go, so that they can worship me. If you refuse, I will punish your country by covering it with frogs. The Nile will be so full of frogs that they will leave it and go into your palace, your bedroom, your bed, the houses of your officials and your people, and even into your ovens and baking pans. They will jump up on you, your people, and your officials.'" The Lord said to Moses, "Tell Aaron to hold out his stick over the rivers, the canals, and the pools, and make frogs come up and cover the

land of Egypt." So Aaron held it out over all the
water, and frogs came out and covered the land.

In the following section we will examine the evidence of
courage in Barack Obama, and it is worthy to note that his
audacity is both active and passive.

The Signs of Courage

1. First, for Barack Obama to defy the prejudice of
   color and compete for his party's nomination as its
   2008 presidential candidate was an admirable act of
   courage.

2. Second, Barack Obama dared to confront the
   weight and popularity of his primaries rival, Hillary
   Clinton, to actively defend his own candidacy. Thus,
   through courage he won the primaries, even against
   the backdrop of his inexperience and character
   assassination by detractors.

3. What was even more audacious was that Barack
   Obama was in the hunt for the presidency, not to
   continue in the routine of the White House, but to
   change what he called "the ways of Washington." And
   when he declared, from the very beginning, that "the
   ways of Washington must change," he was, indeed,
   taking a great risk. The risk was enormous because
   at that time no one could imagine why, how, and
   what change was going to be. When situations like
   the financial crunch came up later, they proved that
   Barack Obama was right, and his shout for change
   was no longer a lonely cry.

4. Moreover, the fact that Barack Obama was not scared by the tragic fate of Martin Luther King Jr., the celebrated American black rights activist who was assassinated by a racist fanatic in 1968, was concrete proof of his passive audacity.

5. Finally, Barack Obama was not in any way intimidated by the many assassination attempts made on him right from the beginning of his 2008 presidential campaign.[45]

Now let us find out the sources of the very strong courage of President Barack Obama.

The Sources of Courage

The courage of Barack Obama originates from two main sources: spiritual and human.

1. The first spiritual source of courage for Barack Obama is his established identity with the number one. As we discussed in chapter 3, he is gifted with the independence, authority, and domination that is characteristic of the number one.

2. The second spiritual source of courage for Barack Obama is his established identity with the number four. He is thus blessed with the strength, endurance, and firmness that are distinctive of the number four.

3. The most obvious human sources of courage for Barack Obama are the circumstances of his birth, youth, and upbringing. By the standards of the United States, Barack Obama was neither born nor bred in comfortable conditions. Besides, both his childhood

in Indonesia and his student life in New York City brought him into contact with many human and social injustices.[46] As a result, he grew up, consciously or unconsciously, with a very revolutionary spirit and a strong determination to change adverse situations into favorable ones. He first sought to change his own conditions of life, and then to assist those whom he considered to be victims of natural and human injustices.

4. Eventually, therefore, Barack Obama's desire for change further enhanced his audacity. For, having nothing to lose, he had nothing to fear in taking risks to change things that needed to be changed.

The following section is a discussion about the use of courage by Barack Obama as a weapon to conquer and rule.

The Power of Courage

1. First, the exemplary courage of Barack Obama not only weakens his opponents but also puts off his detractors. In fact, it boosts his charisma, strength, and credibility. For, having proved that he can face any danger, he, naturally becomes the source of hope and trust in critical times. This is how audacity paved the way of Barack Obama to the White House in 2008, and maintained him in 2012 for another four-year mandate. In fact, he is recognized by the body of voters as a good shepherd. Thus the scriptures say in John 10:8–15,

> All others who came before me are thieves and robbers, but the sheep did not listen to them. I am the gate. Whoever comes in by me will be saved; they

will come in and go out and find pasture. The thief comes only in order to steal, kill, and destroy. I have come in order that you might have life—life in all its fullness. I am the good shepherd, who is willing to die for the sheep. When the hired man, who is not a shepherd and does not own the sheep, sees a wolf coming, he leaves the sheep and runs away; so the wolf snatches the sheep and scatters them. The hired man runs away because he is only a hired man and does not care about the sheep. I am the good shepherd. As the Father knows me and I know the Father, in the same way I know my sheep and they know me. And I am willing to die for them.

2. Second, the audacity of Barack Obama is one of the mighty pillars of his presidency. This is so because he is holding office at a very critical moment in history—when the United States and the whole world are facing severe economic and financial crises, as well as security and environmental challenges. All these problems require timely and effective solutions, and such would include decisions and actions that have not been taken or tested anywhere before. Barack Obama has done a lot, so far, but much still has to be done. These include complete financial and economic recovery, the suppression of terrorist groups, the control of gun abuse in the United States and arms proliferation in the world, and a halt to climate change. In fact, there is no time to waste, and he must take the initiative and assume the responsibility for every act and its consequences.

3. The courage of Barack Obama also enables him to safeguard the heritage, prestige, and supremacy of the United States of America by taking bold steps to maintain the balance of power in favor of the United

States. The continuing standoff between President Barack Obama and the leaders of Iran and North Korea against their nuclear programs is a practical demonstration of his courage and firmness.

4. Nevertheless, audacity is a double-edged knife, and in order that it does not overstep its bounds and break itself, it must take proper doses of wisdom and prudence. This is so because audacity without wisdom is a blind force. Fortunately, Barack Obama does not lack insight and modesty. Therefore, we can rightly conclude that his audacity will work within reasonable limits to serve the causes of freedom, development, justice, peace, and prosperity in America and the whole world.

In chapter 11, we will discuss the plague of gnats as a sacred weapon of Barack Obama.

---

44. A **plague** is a large number of insects, animals, or some other thing that comes into a place and causes great damage.
45. ABC News, October 27, 2008.
46. www.barack-obama-bio.com.

Artwork 12 of 21: Gnat.

This is a small fly with two wings that bites.

CHAPTER ELEVEN

The Plague of Gnats

> So Aaron struck the ground with his stick and all the dust in Egypt was turned into gnats, which covered the people and the animals. The magicians tried to use their magic to make gnats appear, but they failed. There were gnats everywhere.
>
> (Exodus 8:17–18)

THE previous chapter discussed the plague of frogs as the power of courage of Barack Obama. In this chapter we will discuss the plague of gnats, which symbolizes the excellence of Barack Obama.

Background

The power of excellence constitutes intelligence, competence, creativity, and performance. It is the fundamental weapon of every great achiever. Excellence is the means to materialize hope. It is the focal point of admiration, love, and trust. Thus excellence gives power and fame to whoever possesses and uses it.

The Plague of Gnats

Therefore, the excellence of Barack Obama turned his songs of hope and change to shouts of victory in the 2008 and 2012 presidential polls. And this happened because no one, not even the magicians, could imitate his amazing performances. This fulfills what the scripture says in Exodus 8:16–19:

> The Lord said to Moses, "Tell Aaron to strike the ground with his stick and all over the land of Egypt the dust will change into gnats." So Aaron struck the ground with his stick and all the dust in Egypt was turned into gnats, which covered the people and the animals. The magicians tried to use their magic to make gnats appear, but they failed. There were gnats everywhere, and the magicians said to the king, "God has done this!"

Thus, like the plague of gnats, the excellence of Barack Obama surpasses his challengers to win the battles of the White House.

In the section that follows we are going to discuss the evidence of excellence of Barack Obama.

The Signs of Excellence

1. Certainly, the most remarkable signs of excellence in Barack Obama are found in his writings and speeches. In fact, it was the brilliant keynote speech[47] that he delivered at the 2004 Democratic National

Convention in Boston that first put him into the limelight of politics in the United States. The tone and pertinence of that speech foretold that Barack Obama not only had the power to do great things, but could actually be the one to put things right when everything was going wrong. And ever since, his political rallies have always pulled mammoth crowds.

2. Subsequently, in 2006 Barack Obama won a Grammy award for best spoken word for the CD version of his autobiography, *Dreams from My Father*.[48] And in 2008, he won a second Grammy award for best spoken word album for another of his books, titled, *The Audacity of Hope*.[49] These distinctions are, of course, evidence of the very high standards of his works, and these standards are a reflection of his excellence.

3. Also, in 1990 Barack Obama was distinguished as the first African American editor of the renowned *Harvard Law Review*.

4. Furthermore, in 2005 and 2007, *Time* magazine named Barack Obama among the "one hundred most influential people in the world,"[50] and in 2005 *New Statesman* magazine chose him as one of the "ten people who would change the world."[51]

5. Again, in 2008, *Time* magazine chose Barack Obama as "the most famous person in the world." The editors of *Time* magazine wrote, "In one of the craziest elections in American history, Barack Obama overcame a lack of experience, a funny name, two candidates who are political institutions, and the racial divide to become the forty-fourth president of the United States."[52]

6. In 2009, the Nobel Foundation chose Barack Obama as the winner of the Nobel Peace Prize.[53] This was in recognition of his excellent engagement for peace in the world, especially in the Middle East. In fact, according to the Norwegian Nobel Committee, Barack Obama was awarded the prize for his "extraordinary efforts to strengthen international diplomacy and cooperation between peoples."

7. Finally, in 2012 President Barack Obama was again chosen as the *Time* magazine person of the year. In choosing him, the editors of *Time* wrote thus:

> We are in the midst of historic cultural and demographic changes, and Barack Obama is both the symbol and in some ways the architect of this new America. In 2012, he found and forged a new majority, turned weakness into opportunity, and sought, amid great adversity, to create a more perfect union.[54]

The section that follows examines the sources of excellence in Barack Obama.

The Sources of Excellence

The excellence of Barack Obama originates from a combination of spiritual and human factors.

1. On the spiritual plane, Barack Obama has a strong identity with the number one. This gives him the powers of intelligence, wisdom, creativity, and ingenuity. It is so because, as we discussed in chapter 3, the number one symbolizes God, who is the Creator and source of all power.

2. Also, the excellence of Barack Obama is an attribute of the number two. In chapter 4 we concluded that the number four is one of Barack Obama's vital numbers. We also proved that the number two is a direct projection of the number one. This corresponds with what the scriptures say in John 1:1–5: "In the beginning the Word already existed; the Word was with God, and the Word was God. From the very beginning the Word was with God. Through him God made all things; not one thing in all creation was made without him. The Word was the source of life, and this life brought light to humanity. The light shines in the darkness, and the darkness has never put it out." On this position, we affirm that the excellence of Barack Obama is a reflection of divine intelligence and that he is, in fact, an instrument of God.

3. Moreover, Barack Obama's identity with the number three, especially, gives him excellence because the number three has the power of perfect creation, action, and reaction.

4. On the human plane, the superior education and training of Barack Obama greatly enhanced his excellence. Despite his modest background, he actually attended the top schools of his time. They included Punahou preparatory school in Hawaii, Columbia University, and Harvard Law School.

5. Evidently, the legal training of Barack Obama and the competitive nature of the law profession gave him the opportunity to develop and strengthen his power of excellence.

6. Furthermore, Barack Obama's work as a lecturer at the University of Chicago Law School enabled him

to stimulate his intellect, increase his knowledge, and enhance his excellence.

The next section will discuss how Barack Obama uses excellence as a weapon to conquer and dominate from the White House.

The Power of Excellence

1. Excellence builds trust and hope in anyone who is endowed with it; it enhances the credibility and popularity of the one who exercises it. These are the key factors that determine victory in any election that is as free and fair as the polls in the United States. Thus revealed by his excellence, the star of Barack Obama shines so brightly that no one can resist his charm. Therefore, his successive victories in the 2008 and 2012 presidential elections were the results of his excellence.

2. The excellence of Barack Obama enhances his skill in the management of state affairs, implementation of policies, and resolution of differences. Therefore, the weapon of excellence is essential to the realization of his most cherished dreams of a freer America and a more peaceful world.

3. Finally, the greatest merit of his excellence is that Barack Obama is able to take very good initiatives to satisfy the aspirations of the people he governs and to coin the best solutions for problems facing America and the world today. This is evident in his punctual reactions to incidents of terrorist attacks, gun abuse, and natural calamities in the United States. Also, in his last term of office President Barack Obama

is actually taking steps to promote human liberties, social justice, and universal health care in the United States. Finally, his diplomatic engagements, especially with Russia, China, and Europe, are focused on improving peace and security, and promoting free trade and a safe environment for the benefit of the whole world.

In chapter 12, we will discuss the plague of flies as a sacred weapon of Barack Obama.

47. Barack Obama, *The Essential Barack Obama: The Grammy Award–Winning Recordings of Barack Obama* (New York: Random House, 2008).
48. www.barack-obama-bio.com.
49. Ibid.
50. Ibid.
51. Ibid.
52. *Time*, New York, December 17, 2008.
53. Nobel Foundation Awards, 2009.
54. *Time*, New York, December 19, 2012.

Artwork 13 of 21: Fly. This is a small flying insect with two
wings that is usually found around rotting matter.

CHAPTER TWELVE

The Plague of Flies

The Lord sent great swarms of flies into the king's palace and the houses of his officials. The whole land of Egypt was brought to ruin by the flies.

(Exodus 8:24)

THE previous chapter discussed the plague of gnats, which represents the excellence of Barack Obama. The subject of this chapter is the plague of flies, which stands for the love of Barack Obama.

Background

Love is the deepest of all mysteries; it is the greatest of all laws, and the strongest of all powers. It is the reason why God created man and gave him power. In Genesis 1:26–29, the scripture says,

> Then God said, "And now we will make human beings; they will be like us and resemble us. They will have power over the fish, the birds, and all animals, domestic and wild, large and small." So God created human beings, making them to be like himself. He created them male and female, blessed them, and said, "Have many children so that your descendants will live all over the earth and bring it under their control. I am putting you in charge of the fish, the birds, and all the wild animals. I have provided all kinds of grain and all kinds of fruit for you to eat; but for all the wild animals and for all the birds I have provided grass and leafy plants for food"—and it was done.

Our love for one another is a reflection of God's great love for us. Thus in Romans 13:8–10 it is written,

> Be under obligation to no one—the only obligation you have is to love one another. Whoever does this has obeyed the Law. The commandments "Do not commit adultery; do not commit murder; do not steal; do not desire what belongs to someone else"—all these, and any others besides, are summed up in the one command, "love your neighbor as you love yourself." If you love someone you will never do them wrong; to love, then, is to obey the whole Law.

Then in John 13:34–35, Jesus Christ says, "And now I give you a new commandment: love one another. As I have loved you, so you must love one another. If you have love for one another, then everyone will know that you are my disciples." And in John 15:12–13, he says, "My commandment is this: love one another just as I love you. The greatest love a person can have for his friends is to give his life for them."

Therefore, love evokes equality, generosity, tolerance, justice, and the protection of life and nature. It is the foundation of progress, peace, and security in the world.

The Plague of Flies

In Exodus 8:20–25, it is written,

> The Lord said to Moses, "Early tomorrow morning go and meet the king as he goes to the river, and tell him that the Lord says, 'Let my people go so that they can worship me. I warn you that if you refuse, I will punish you by sending flies on you, your officials, and your people. The houses of the Egyptians will be full of flies, and the ground will be covered with them. But I will spare the region of Goshen, where my people live, so that there will be no flies there. I will do this so that you will know that I, the Lord, am at work in this land. I will make a distinction between my people and your people. This miracle will take place tomorrow.'" The Lord sent great swarms of flies into the king's palace and the houses of his officials. The whole land of Egypt was brought to ruin by the flies. Then the king called for Moses and Aaron and said, "Go and offer sacrifices to your God here in this country."

The swarming of flies into the palace also symbolizes the communion between the rich and the poor, religious and atheist, Republicans and Democrats, and blacks, whites, and Latinos to elect and reelect Barack Obama as president of the United States. In fact, this solidarity was originally brought about in 2008 by the economic downturn and terrorist activities that threatened everybody. In the next section we will examine the signs of love in Barack Obama.

The Signs of Love

1. It has been reported that, as a child growing up in Indonesia, Barack Obama was shocked by the simultaneous luxury and distressing poverty of that tropical country. Later, as a student at Columbia University, he was marked by the inescapable social tension in New York City. And in Chicago he spent three years working to help poor South Side residents cope with unemployment difficulties.[55] As much as his emotions demonstrated his power of love, so also the various circumstances enhanced his humanity.

2. When Barack Obama graduated from the renowned Harvard Law School, he turned down, surprisingly, a prestigious judicial clerkship and returned to Chicago to practice civil-rights law. This was to empower him to defend victims of housing and employment discrimination. There, he also worked on legislation in favor of voting rights for all.[56] In fact, these are unquestionable signs of love.

3. Barack Obama's political platform,[57] in favor of jobs, housing, security, health, environment protection, and international dialogue, is a faithful reflection of his love for humanity. He does not put up a kindly face and speak the language of love only as a campaign strategy—since his youth, humanity has been an inherent part of his life.

In the next section we will discuss the sources from which Barack Obama gets the power of love.

The Sources of Love

The profound humanity of Barack Obama derives from the numbers two, eight, and five.

1. The number two, symbol of the Son of God and Savior of the world, gives Barack Obama the powers of redemption. Because of this, the well-being of mankind becomes both his personal concern and most urgent mission.

2. The number eight, symbol of the double square, makes Barack Obama a keen advocate and practitioner of the Golden Rule—"Love your neighbor as yourself." This corresponds to what the scripture says in 1 John 3:11–18:

> The message you heard from the beginning is this: we must love one another. We must not be like Cain; he belonged to the evil one and murdered his own brother, Abel. Why did Cain murder him? Because the things he himself did were wrong, but the things his brother did were right. So do not be surprised, my brothers and sisters, if the people of the world hate you. We know that we have left death and come over into life; we know it because we love our brothers and sisters. Whoever does not love is still under the power of death. All who hate others are murderers, and you know that murderers have not got eternal life in them. This is how we know what love is: Christ gave his life for us. We too, then, ought to give our lives for our brothers and sisters! Rich people, who see a brother or sister in need, yet close their hearts against them, cannot claim that they love God. My

children, our love should not be just words and talk; it must be true love, which shows itself in action.

Besides, in 1 John, chapter 4, verses 19 to 21, it is written,

> We love because God first loved us. If we say we love God, but hate our brothers and sisters, we are liars. For people cannot love God, whom they have not seen, if they do not love their brothers and sisters, whom they have seen. The command that Christ has given us is this: all who love God must love their brother or sister also.

3. The number five, symbol of perfection in the pentagonal dimensions (body, mind, heart, spirit, and soul) of human existence, inflames him with love, tolerance, and solicitude. And these are the virtues that strive for peace, harmony, and well-being, within people and in the society. This explains why Barack Obama is very concerned with creating humane conditions for people in America and everywhere in the world. And he acts with neither pride nor prejudice.

4. Nevertheless, the humanity of Barack Obama cannot be explained, exclusively, by spiritual factors. It is evident that the circumstances of his birth, childhood, and education contributed enormously to the germination of his spiritual seed of love. In fact, his humble birth, racial stigmatization, and early exposure to human poverty and social inequality in Jakarta, New York City, and Chicago could not leave him indifferent to the plight and misfortunes of people, who like him were sometimes placed at the margins of society.

5. Moreover, his training as a lawyer—at the distinguished Harvard Law School—gives him not only an extraordinary skill to defend the cause of justice, but also the sympathy to assist those who cannot pay for justice. It is known that the clients of Barack Obama were not those who could pay the fees but, in fact, those who were in need of justice. Thus he equally defended the weak and the strong, as well as the poor and the rich.

In the next section we will discuss how the power of love enabled Barack Obama to accede to the prestigious presidency of the United States.

The Power of Love

1. The unprecedented financial crunch that started in the United States in July 2008, and the resulting economic downturn and real-estate mortgage crisis, actually pleaded for Barack Obama. That was because the humanitarian argument at that time heavily outweighed the other considerations, such as terrorism, war, and diplomacy. In fact, with his having proved his deep and constant love of others, it was but natural for the ballot box to weigh in his favor.

2. Moreover, the disposition of Barack Obama to defend the underprivileged, and to promote social justice, equality, and collective well-being, put him in alignment with the necessity and hope to eliminate such global miseries as disease, war, poverty, hunger, and insecurity. It is for this reason that he came to symbolize hope—hope for change, hope for America, and hope for the world.

3. The humanity of Barack Obama moves him to take fast, bold steps to protect the helpless classes of society. These include the protection of old jobs and the creation of new ones, as well as the provision of Social Security and health insurance. These matters, among others, made up the package of his campaign promises to the American people; and he has fought to fulfill them. In fact, on March 21, 2010, President Barack Obama won a landmark victory of 219 votes against 212 in the US House of Representatives to pass his controversial health-care bill.[58] Furthermore, his vigorous campaign to increase taxes for the rich agrees with the scriptures in 1 John 3:16–18:

> This is how we know what love is: Christ gave his life for us. We too, then, ought to give our lives for our brothers and sisters! Rich people, who see a brother or sister in need, yet close their hearts against them, cannot claim that they love God. My children, our love should not be just words and talk; it must be true love, which shows itself in action.

4. Furthermore, Barack Obama is working hard to address the very vexing problems of drugs, crime, and insecurity, both in the United States and around the world. In America, he is actively campaigning against uncontrolled gun rights because of the rising incidents of gun abuse in recent times. Thus, reacting on March 23, 2012, to the shooting of a teenager in Florida, President Barack Obama said, "I think Trayvon's parents are right to expect that all of us as Americans are going to take this with the seriousness it deserves, and we are going to get to the bottom of exactly what happened."[59] Again, following the brutal shooting of twenty pupils and seven teachers at an elementary school in Newtown, Connecticut, in

December 2012, Barack Obama signed twenty-three executive orders on January 16, 2013. The measures were made to prevent gun violence. They placed a control on the sale of arms to prevent criminals from getting access to them, and they also placed a ban on "weapons of war" and "assault weapons."[60] Although the National Rifle Association is strongly fighting to frustrate his efforts, it is expected that the machinery of this powerful association will eventually crumble against the holy weapons of Barack Obama.

5. On the global front, President Barack Obama is definitely at war against terrorism—especially in the Arab world—which is a major threat to life, property, peace, and stability in the world. Armed conflicts, piracy, rebellions, and dictatorships still exist in many parts of the world, aggravating poverty, disease, and hunger. In most of these areas, including Syria, Sudan, and the Democratic Republic of the Congo, human conditions are unbearable. The real solution is not the supply of medicaments, food, and peacekeeping forces, but the elimination of the fundamental causes of human conflicts. These include ignorance, greed, corruption, hatred, revenge, and intolerance. And, in fact, these evils can be eradicated without so much money.

6. Surely, Barack Obama is not unmindful of these. Thus, speaking to the world from the Brandenburg Gate in Berlin in Germany on June 19, 2013, he launched a vigorous campaign to reduce the global stock of arms. He pledged to work with the Russian president to effect the reduction of Russian and American long-range nuclear weapons by one-third. And as he continues to address the issues at stake, the world will finally experience the great power of love.

This is the power that breaks every barrier, as the Berlin Wall was broken, and unites people together, as Jesus Christ unites us to God. Thus the scripture says, in Romans 8:31–39,

> In view of all this, what can we say? If God is for us, who can be against us? Certainly not God, who did not even keep back his own Son, but offered him for us all! He gave us his Son—will he not also freely give us all things? Who will accuse God's chosen people? God himself declares them not guilty! Who, then, will condemn them? Not Christ Jesus, who died, or rather, who was raised to life and is at the right-hand side of God, pleading with him for us! Who, then, can separate us from the love of Christ? Can trouble do it or hardship or persecution or hunger or poverty or danger or death? As the scripture says, "For your sake we are in danger of death at all times; we are treated like sheep that are going to be slaughtered."

No, in all these things we have complete victory through him who loved us! For I am certain that nothing can separate us from his love: neither death nor life, neither angels nor other heavenly rulers or powers, neither the present nor the future, neither the world above nor the world below—there is nothing in all creation that will ever be able to separate us from the love of God that is ours through Christ Jesus our Lord.

In chapter 13, we will discuss the plague of the death of the animals as a sacred weapon of Barack Obama.

55. www.barack-obama-bio.com.
56. Ibid.
57. Barack Obama, *Change We Can Believe In: Barack Obama's Plan to Renew America's Promise* (New York: Crown Publishing, 2009).
58. BBC News, March 21, 2010.
59. BBC News, March 23, 2012.
60. CNN News, January 16, 2013.

Artwork 14 of 21: Head of Bull and Cross.
This is the symbol of the dead animals.

CHAPTER THIRTEEN

The Death of the Animals

> I will punish you by sending a terrible disease
> on all your animals—your horses, donkeys,
> camels, cattle, sheep, and goats. The next
> day the Lord did as he had said, and all the
> animals of the Egyptians died, but not one of
> the animals of the Israelites died.
>
> **(Exodus 9:3, 6)**

WE discussed the plague of flies in chapter 12. In this chapter we will talk about the plague of the death of the animals, which symbolizes the uniqueness of Barack Obama.

Background

The gift of uniqueness is what makes everybody different from everyone else. To be one of a type, and to live and express that uniqueness without pride, shame, or fear, is an important quality. In fact, particularity invokes curiosity, and sometimes awe and fear.

The Plague of the Death of the Animals

In Exodus 9:1–6, the scriptures say,

> The Lord said to Moses, "Go to the king and tell him that the Lord, the God of the Hebrews, says, 'Let my people go, so that they may worship me. If you again refuse to let them go, I will punish you by sending a terrible disease on all your animals—your horses, donkeys, camels, cattle, sheep, and goats. I will make a distinction between the animals of the Israelites and those of the Egyptians, and no animal that belongs to the Israelites will die. I, the Lord, have set tomorrow as the time when I will do this.'" The next day the Lord did as he had said, and all the animals of the Egyptians died, but not one of the animals of the Israelites died.

As the plague of the death of the animals, the uniqueness of Barack Obama was one of the holy weapons that he employed in the November 4, 2008, battle for the White House. His particularity was found in his ideas, age, and race. He was the only African American, so far, who had not been stopped on the way to the White House. On the contrary, he stopped the others, who unlike him, all "died" like the animals.

In the next section we will examine the elements of the uniqueness of Barack Obama.

The Signs of Uniqueness

1. First, the political slogan of Barack Obama, "Change We Need, Change We Can," was at the same time unique and doubtful. In fact, when he said in one

of his speeches that "the ways of Washington must change,"[61] no one could understand, at that time, how and why America was going to change.

2. Second, the color of Barack Obama is another feature of his particularity. Certainly, he is not the only American who is black or of mixed origin, but he is the first of his type to have bypassed political, social, and racial interests to stand and defend America as one nation. The following is an excerpt of the keynote speech that Barack Obama gave at the 2004 Democratic National Convention in Boston:

> There's not a liberal America and a conservative America. There's the United States of America. We worship an awesome God in the blue states, and we don't like federal agents poking around our libraries in the red states. We coach Little League in the blue states, and have gay friends in the red states. There are patriots who opposed the war, and patriots who supported it. We are one people, all of us pledging allegiance to the Stars and Stripes, all of us defending the United States of America.[62]

Furthermore, in the same speech, he said,

> And it lives on in those Americans—young and old, rich and poor, black and white, Latino and Asian and Native American, gay and straight—who are tired of a politics that divides us and want to recapture the sense of common purpose that we had when John Kennedy was president of the United States of America.[62]

3. Third, the particularity of Barack Obama paved the way for another distinction—the fact of him being

the first-ever African American to win a party's nomination for the presidency of the United States of America. That alone made history, which drew to him keen curiosity and admiration.

4. Fourth, the age of Barack Obama was another characteristic of his particularity. At the time of his first election as president of the United States, he was forty-seven years old. His age put him, strategically, at the crossroads of the younger and the older generations of people in the United States.

5. Fifth, in 2008 Barack Obama had been a US senator for only four years. And that very short career made him essentially a novice in the political arena of the United States. Interestingly, however, that aroused not only skepticism but also admiration, drawing more curiosity and attention to him.

In the next section we will examine the sources from which Barack Obama draws his uniqueness.

The Sources of Uniqueness

1. First, in the spiritual plane, his particularity is determined by the number one and the number two. The number one is the first and the only one—no other number comes before it. The number one is, therefore, unique and represents someone or something that is different from all others.

2. Second, the uniqueness of the number one is projected in the number two. Thus the operation of $1 + 1 = 2$ yields the number two. The number two is the symbol of the only Son of God—Jesus Christ. Therefore,

the uniqueness of Barack Obama comes from the spiritual plane as a result of his double identity with the number one and the number two. This is in conformity with the scriptures in John 1:14: "The Word became a human being and, full of grace and truth, lived among us. We saw his glory, the glory which he received as the Father's only Son." Also, in John 3:16, the scripture says, "For God loved the world so much that he gave his only Son, so that everyone who believes in him may not die but have eternal life." And in John 14:10–11, it is written,

> "Do you not believe, Philip, that I am in the Father and the Father is in me? The words that I have spoken to you," Jesus said to his disciples, "do not come from me. The Father, who remains in me, does his own work. Believe me when I say that I am in the Father and the Father is in me. If not, believe because of the things I do."

So Barack Obama, being empowered by the number two, is the one and the only one like him, as Jesus Christ is the one and the only Son of God.

In the human sphere, the particularity of Barack Obama derives from two factors—his parentage and his youthful experiences.

1. First, Barack Obama was born of a black father and a white mother. This makes him neither black nor white, but a blend of black and white. This fact is not peculiar to him alone, but as has already been mentioned, Barack Obama is the only one of his type who has ever climbed so high on the ladder of politics to defend the diversity of the American people.

2. Second, the family background of Barack Obama, his life as a youth in Indonesia, and his student experiences in New York City together played a key role in making him a unique thinker and actor. In fact, his family condition was not so comfortable, and with that, he could grow up only with the single hope for and determination to change.

3. Finally, it is reported that Barack Obama once described Indonesia as "simultaneously lush, and a harrowing exposure to tropical poverty." This experience of social misery, coupled with that of social tension that he had as a student in New York City, was indeed obnoxious and revolting. Definitely, these experiences helped to develop the seed of change that was already sowed in him by the number one.

In the next section we will see how Barack Obama uses uniqueness as a holy weapon to conquer and exercise political power in the United States and worldwide.

The Power of Uniqueness

As already has been explained, particularity sparks curiosity and draws attention to itself. Therefore, because of his uniqueness Barack Obama became a subject of curiosity since 2006, when he first declared his intention to run for president of the United States.

With curiosity, attention became increasingly focused on him. Everybody wanted to find out about his character and his merits. And so the world came to discover that Barack Obama was not a political adventurer but rather a dependable candidate, capable of leading the United States and the whole world through contemporary challenges.

Having discovered his merits and capacity, Americans began to give Barack Obama their massive support. And with this came the multitude of votes that decided his overwhelming victory in the 2008 ballot. Thus he became the forty-fourth president of the United States, and the first-ever African American to occupy the White House.

When Barack Obama said in one of his speeches that "the ways of Washington must change," no one understood at that time how and why politics in the White House had to change. However, when the capitalism of the United States went mad and her financial system began to collapse, many people began to find reason in the slogan of change. Barack Obama thus became synonymous with change, as change itself had become the hope of the people.

Besides, some people had already anticipated change, especially in American diplomacy. The reason was that the diplomatic dictatorship and arrogance of former President George Walker Bush had made the United States very unpopular abroad and brought her image to the lowest level ever. Therefore, Barack Obama's slogan of change was received with increasing interest and relief.

Currently, the uniqueness of Barack Obama puts him squarely at the crossroads of all generations and races in the United States of America. This makes him receptive to different ideas and alert to the problems of different peoples and interest groups. This comprehensive sympathy ensures that his administration is both balanced and fair for all citizens and residents of the United States.

Furthermore, the particularity of Barack Obama enables him to work out unique decisions and take unprecedented actions to overcome the challenges of his administration—especially to overhaul the economy and improve upon the well-being of the people. In fact, the end of the current financial and economic crisis would benefit not only America but also the entire world, given that the United States is the catalyst of the global financial and commodity markets.

Surely, initiatives by Barack Obama are not limited to the economy alone, but also embrace America's diplomatic relations and foreign engagements. The beneficial outcome of these is the evident improvement of the image of the United States abroad. This is followed, naturally, by the elimination of "Americano-phobia" and the cultivation of mutual diplomatic respect to benefit world peace and stability.

Finally, the particularity of Barack Obama, combined with his sense of sympathy, receptivity, and tolerance, is a formidable force that shapes a new America—more prosperous and stronger than ever before. This new nation, born again, is expected not to oppress but to lead the other nations of the world. For the practice that stronger nations protect, rather than plunder, the weaker ones is the very particularity of the Barack Obama world.

In chapter 14, we will discuss the plague of boils as a sacred weapon of Barack Obama.

---

61. Barack Obama, *The Essential Barack Obama: The Grammy Award–Winning Recordings of Barack Obama* (New York: Random House, 2008).

62. Ibid.

Artwork 15 of 21: Boils. These are painful infected swellings under the skin that are full of pus.

CHAPTER FOURTEEN

The Plague of Boils

So they got some ashes and stood before the king; Moses threw them into the air, and they produced boils that became open sores on the people and the animals. The magicians were not able to appear before Moses, because they were covered with boils, like all other Egyptians.

(Exodus 9:10–11)

IN the previous chapter we discussed the plague of the death of the animals as symbolizing the uniqueness of Barack Obama. Our discussion in this chapter will focus on the plague of boils, which symbolizes the charm of Barack Obama.

Background

Charm not only is one of the many effects of beauty, but it is probably the most impressive. Beauty in all its facets is the source of attraction and wonderment. This magnetic radiance, charm, is emitted by true beauty—beauty that is neither temporary nor superficial; beauty that is both profound and all-inclusive. These are the beauty of the heart, the beauty of the tongue, the beauty of motion, the beauty of action, the beauty of conduct, and the beauty of the body—all expressing the beauty of God. The manifestation of charm or charismatic magnetism conditions the thinking, feelings, and reactions of other people. It wields enormous power, and it sometime earns unconditional support and allegiance.

The Plague of Boils

In Exodus 9:8–11, it is written,

> Then the Lord said to Moses and Aaron, "Take a few handfuls of ashes from a furnace; Moses shall throw them into the air in front of the king. They will spread out like fine dust over all the land of Egypt, and everywhere they will produce boils that become open sores on the people and the animals." So they got some ashes and stood before the king; Moses threw them into the air, and they produced boils that became open sores on the people and the animals. The magicians were not able to appear before Moses, because they were covered with boils, like all other Egyptians.

Thus, like a plague of boils, the exceptional charm of Barack Obama outshines the radiance of his challengers and makes them eyesores.

In the next section we will examine the evidence of charm in Barack Obama.

The Signs of Charm

The charm of Barack Obama, which has already been entrenched in the new concept of "Obamamania," is a true reflection of his multifarious brilliance.

1. The charm of Barack Obama is evident in the elegance of his body, the fluency of his voice, and his smartness.

2. The charm of Barack Obama is evident in his aptitude, confidence, liveliness, and sense of humor.

3. It is the charm of Barack Obama that swelled the crowds in all his rallies, provoking high waves of hysteria, ecstasy, and sympathy.

In the following section we will find out the sources from which Barack Obama derives his exceptional magnetic power.

The Sources of Charm

Essentially, the charm of Barack Obama comes from two complementary sources—the spiritual sources and the human sources. The spiritual sources are his strong identities with the numbers one, three, four, five, and eight. And as we shall see, these spiritual sources feed the material sources to realize his power of charm.

1. The number one, the symbol of the Godhead, conditions his extraordinary intelligence, creativity, and brilliance. These great virtues of Barack Obama all combine to make him a powerfully charming personality.

2. The number three, as the symbol of perfect action and reaction, enhances the smartness, oratory, and humor of Barack Obama. In fact, his attitudes in speech and dressing are a curious combination of humor and importance, as well as seriousness and simplicity. The dexterity of his looks, movements, and pauses adds even more. And these make him very attractive and fascinating to his audiences.

3. The number four, as the symbol of material perfection, forms the physique and elegance of Barack Obama. In fact, his height of 1.87 meters is very standard, and his size is just moderate—between slimness and fatness. Besides, his dark hair, now becoming gray, and his light complexion are lost between black and white. All together, he is a remarkable representative of the multiracial American society.

4. The excellence, integrity, and humanity of Barack Obama come from the number five, as the symbol of spiritual empowerment and harmony in the pentagonal dimensions (body, heart, mind, spirit, and soul) of human existence. Thus, his excellence is rewarded with admiration, his integrity with trust, and his humanity with love; and whoever loves is attracted to the one he or she loves.

5. The number eight, which symbolizes double stability and conformity between divine and human qualities, gives Barack Obama confidence, serenity, conviviality, and liveliness.

6. Finally, the charm of Barack Obama is also boosted by his sincerity, frankness, and simplicity. In fact, during the 2008 campaign for the presidency of the United States, he openly confessed his youthful

experimentation with drugs, to the surprise of many and at the risk of losing his credibility.

In the next section we will discover how Barack Obama uses his charm as a sacred weapon to conquer and exercise power.

The Power of Charm

Evidently, the charm of Barack Obama was the ultimate factor that decided his first victory, in 2008, in the campaign for the White House.

1. It was the charm of Barack Obama that swelled the crowds in all his rallies, provoking high waves of hysteria, ecstasy, and sympathy with his political plan. By pulling huge crowds to his rallies, his charm gave him the opportunity, every time, to address, to impress, and to convince the greatest number of voters.

2. The charm of Barack Obama earned him the endorsement of several musical icons, Hollywood stars, and editors of distinguished media houses, like the *New York Times*. By his charm he also won the support of respectable statesmen and corporate magnates. For example, his candidacy for the White House was publicly endorsed by former Republican Secretary of State Colin Powell. Former US President Bill Clinton and many other celebrities—such as George Clooney, Bob Dylan, and Eddie Murphy— all endorsed and sponsored the candidacy of Barack Obama during the 2008 presidential campaign.[63]

3. With overwhelming support, Barack Obama disregarded public funding and financed his 2008 campaign exclusively from private sources. In fact, he raised the colossal sum of over $605 million,[64] about five times the amount that was available to his Republican challenger, John McCain. In 2012 the Obama campaign was also the highest fund-raiser.

4. The charm of Barack Obama also brought many volunteers who took part in the organization of his campaign and the running of the ballot proper, in both 2008 and 2012.

5. Therefore, it is right to conclude that the great charm of Barack Obama gave him the fabulous number of votes by which he brilliantly won his ticket to the White House in 2008 and his reelection in 2012.

6. Meanwhile, the charm of Barack Obama is all intact, and it continues to earn him admiration, loyalty, and collaboration from the various political forces, social classes, and racial groups in the United States of America. This particular synergy enables him to work out and implement effective and equitable solutions to the different problems that America and the world face today.

7. On the international scene, the charm of Barack Obama facilitates his diplomatic intercourse with other world powers—like Russia, China, and Europe—to ease tensions and prevent wars.

8. However, as far as leadership is concerned, charm has a threshold limit, beyond which it would have a negative effect. First, charm must be moderated with humility and receptivity so that leadership does

not turn to dictatorship and, hence, lose track of its purpose. Second, charm must be tied to sincerity, rationality, and integrity. This is to ensure that it does not backfire, such as when the people see their leader as a god, capable of performing miracles and doing the impossible. These complementary virtues certainly are not lacking in Barack Obama; therefore, his charm will continue to assist him in the discharge of his functions and the attainment of his dreams for America and the world.

9. Finally, the charm of Barack Obama, which had given birth to the spirit of "Obamamania," again conquered the American electorate in 2012. The second victory of Barack Obama gave him four more years to finalize his plan for change and, hence, attain his national and universal missions in the White House.

In chapter 15, we will discuss the plague of hail as a sacred weapon of Barack Obama.

---

63. *New York Times*, New York City, October 23, 2008.
64. *Washington Post*, Washington, DC, November 20, 2008.

Artwork 16 of 21: Hailstones. These are small blocks of ice
that fall like rain.

CHAPTER FIFTEEN

The Plague of Hail

So Moses raised his stick towards the sky, and the Lord sent thunder and hail, and lightning struck the ground. The Lord sent a heavy hailstorm, with lightning flashing to and fro. It was the worst storm that Egypt has ever known in all its history. All over Egypt the hail struck down everything in the open, including all the people and all the animals. It beat down all the plants in the field and broke all the trees.

(Exodus 9:23–25)

THE previous chapter was about the plague of boils as symbolizing the charm of Barack Obama. Our discussion in this chapter will be on the plague of hail, which represents the oratory of Barack Obama.

Background

The scriptures say, in John1:1–5,

> In the beginning the Word already existed; the
> Word was with God, and the Word was God.
> From the very beginning the Word was with
> God. Through him God made all things; not
> one thing in all creation was made without him.
> The Word was the source of life, and this life
> brought light to humanity. The light shines in the
> darkness, and the darkness has never put it out.

The word is the carrier of both life and light, and through the word everything is made possible. Thus, in Matthew 5:14–16, it is written, "You are the light for the whole world. A city built on a hill cannot be hidden. No one lights a lamp and puts it under a bowl; instead he puts it on the lamp stand, where it gives light for everyone in the house. In the same way your light must shine before people, so that they will see the good things you do and praise your Father in heaven."

Therefore, private wishes, desires, and plans may be kept secret; but ideas, talents, skills, and plans that concern or affect other people must be communicated and promoted. This is so that in the end the vote seeker may faithfully reveal his capacity, to enable the voters to freely make their choice. The word, therefore, is the power that reveals other powers. And God himself is made known and manifests through his Word—Jesus Christ. Thus the scripture says in John 1–18, "No one has ever seen God. The only Son, who is the same as God and is at the Father's side, he has made him known." Oratory, the power of the word, is the talent that reveals other talents. It is the tool of faithful communication to affirm oneself; it is the instrument of effective persuasion to convince others. Besides, oratory possesses a magnetic, if not a bewitching, power. This is the reason why it invokes admiration and confers charismatic powers on anyone who has the talent and mastery of the word.

The Plague of Hail

In Exodus 9:22–25, 27–28, the scriptures say,

> Then the Lord said to Moses, "Raise your hand towards the sky, and hail will fall over the whole land of Egypt—on the people, the animals, and all the plants in the fields." So Moses raised his stick towards the sky, and the Lord sent thunder and hail, and lightning struck the ground. The Lord sent a heavy hailstorm, with lightning flashing to and fro. It was the worst storm that Egypt has ever known in all its history. All over Egypt the hail struck down everything in the open, including all the people and all the animals. It beat down all the plants in the field and broke all the trees. The king sent for Moses and Aaron and said, "This time I have sinned; the Lord is in the right, and my people are in the wrong. Pray to the Lord! We have had enough of this thunder and hail! I promise to let you go; you don't have to stay here any longer."

Thus, like the plague of hail, the oratory of Barack Obama struck America and broke his opponents. The people were overwhelmed and "allowed" him into the White House.

In the next section we will examine evidence of the oratory of Barack Obama.

The Signs of Oratory

1. First, the oratory of Barack Obama won him two Grammy awards—one in 2006 for best spoken word for the CD version of his autobiography, *Dreams from My Father*, and the other in 2008, for best spoken word album for his book *The Audacity of Hope*.

2. Second, as has been mentioned before, it was the very powerful and captivating speech[65] that Barack Obama delivered at the 2004 Democratic National Convention in Boston that projected him as a credible political actor and a worthy contender for the White House.

3. Finally, during the 2008 presidential campaign Barack Obama stunned both his fans and his challengers with his beautiful rhetoric and smart gestures; his serenity was profound, and his confidence was unquenchable. In fact, he remained steadfast, even when his character and integrity were under attack by his opponents and detractors.

The aforementioned facts are all vibrant signs of the power of oratory of Barack Obama. In the next section we will discover the sources from which he gets this power.

The Sources of Oratory

The unequaled oratory of Barack Obama has both spiritual and material sources. The spiritual sources derive from his identity with the numbers one, three, four, and five.

1. The number one, symbolizing the Creator, endows Barack Obama with the powers of creativity, confidence, and authority. Thus he has absolute command both on his speeches and on his audiences.

2. The number three, symbolizing perfect action, reaction, and creation, provides Barack Obama with the merits of correctness, conciseness, clarity, and coherence—both in speech and in writing.

3. The number four, symbolizing material perfection and fixity, endows Barack Obama with strength, vigor, firmness, tone, and serenity, both in writing and in speech.

4. The number five, symbolizing human perfection, endows Barack Obama with the qualities of fluency, vigor, conviviality, and humor.

Besides, there are also human and material factors that account for the extraordinary oratory of Barack Obama.

1. First, his professional activity as a lawyer, and then as a teacher at the University of Chicago Law School, greatly enhanced his oratory. This is obvious, because legal advocacy and teaching are two professions that require regular research, thinking, writing, and talking. Moreover, these professions keep their practitioners constantly in contact and interaction with the public. Therefore, the brilliance of Barack Obama as a writer and orator is a logical continuation of his inborn talents, perfected through study and practice.

2. Moreover, the sympathy of Barack Obama for the underprivileged, and his constant desire to serve

them, made him always to be vocal—and sometimes vociferous—in defense of social rights, equity, and the welfare of the poor. This emotional dynamism, of course, went further to amplify both his tone and his fluency.

3. Finally, it is evident that the very early exposure of Barack Obama to social injustice, especially in Jakarta, New York City, and Chicago, did as much to stimulate his mind as to affect his emotions. That made him to be revolutionary and, especially, vocal in favor of the less-advantaged people of society.

In the next section we will see how Barack Obama uses the weapon of oratory to conquer and exercise political power.

The Power of Oratory

Definitely, oratory is one of the greatest virtues, and probably the most powerful weapon, that Barack Obama has. It is a weapon that he has used, and uses often, either to lure voters or to beat his opponents.

1. First, the oratory of Barack Obama enabled him in 2008 to reveal his personality, competence, and credibility. Eventually, he became the man to beat. And finally, the ballot proved that he was the right captain to steer the US ship through the turbulence of the financial crunch and economic downturn, unemployment, insecurity, and climate change to a safe landing in prosperity, justice, and security.

2. Second, during the presidential debates in 2008 and 2012,[66] the rhetorical efficacy of Barack Obama and his indomitable serenity crushed both the strengths

and the assaults of his opponents—Senator John McCain and Governor Mitt Romney, respectively.

3. Third, the clarity, rationality, and relevance of the speeches of Barack Obama to the prevailing crises were so strong that they not only discouraged his detractors but also enticed the electorate. The viability of his plan for change thus became unquestionable. And following the conviction of the electorate were the overwhelming votes that decided his successive victories in 2008 and 2012.

4. Fourth, the very brilliant arguments, bewitching speeches, and audacious serenity of Barack Obama give him formidable strength and charismatic power. These not only enhance his performance in the polls, but also boost his standing as a statesman with the duty to defend the United States and to influence the world.

5. Fifth, the oratory of Barack Obama enables him to communicate and to interact effectively with both his opponents and his collaborators. This, in turn, creates the necessary synergy for initiative, action, and attainment.

6. In addition, the oratory of Barack Obama helps him to persuade, convince, and gain popular support for his ambitious plans for political, social, and economic change. It also enables him to get the essential backing to reinvent America's diplomacy and to pave new grounds for stability and security in the world.

7. However, in order not to mislead the people, oratory must be matched with realism, rationality, and sincerity. Besides, good doses of patience, prudence,

and silence are very necessary to avoid premature pronouncements and public blunders. Definitely, these virtues are not wanting in Barack Obama, and there is no doubt that he will always be able to combine them for effective and beneficial use. Thus, on November 6, 2012, the oratory of Barack Obama opened his way to a second term of office in the White House.[67]

In chapter 16, we will discuss the plague of locusts as a sacred weapon of Barack Obama.

---

65. Barack Obama, *The Essential Barack Obama: The Grammy Award–Winning Recordings of Barack Obama* (New York: Random House, 2008).

66. CNN Television Broadcast, October 17, 2012.

67. BBC News, November 7, 2012.

Artwork 17 of 21: Locust. This is a large insect that flies in large groups, destroying all crops and plants along their way.

CHAPTER SIXTEEN

The Plague of Locusts

So Moses raised his stick and the Lord caused a wind from the east to blow on the land all that day and all that night. By morning it had brought the locusts. They came in swarms and settled over the whole country. It was the largest swarm of locusts that had ever been seen or that ever would be seen again. They covered the ground until it was black with them; they ate everything that the hail had left, including all the fruit on the trees. Not a green thing was left on any tree or plant in all the land of Egypt.

(Exodus 10:13–15)

THE last chapter was about the plague of hail as symbolizing the oratory of Barack Obama. In this chapter we will discuss the plague of locusts, which symbolizes the diligence of Barack Obama.

Background

Diligence harnesses talent and uses its competence for effective and constructive achievement. Power without diligence is useless, if not dangerous, in the hands of any human being. Therefore, only diligence, the scrupulous commitment to work, can ensure total success and safety in every enterprise.

The Plague of Locusts

The scriptures say in Exodus 10:12–15,

> Then the Lord said to Moses, "Raise your hand over the land of Egypt to bring the locusts. They will come and eat everything that grows, everything that has survived the hail." So Moses raised his stick and the Lord caused a wind from the east to blow on the land all that day and all that night. By morning it had brought the locusts. They came in swarms and settled over the whole country. It was the largest swarm of locusts that had ever been seen or that ever would be seen again. They covered the ground until it was black with them; they ate everything that the hail had left, including all the fruit on the trees. Not a green thing was left on any tree or plant in all the land of Egypt.

Like the plague of locusts, Barack Obama and his volunteers swarmed the whole of the United States with massive communication campaigns—rallies, television, radio, billboards, and newspapers—in both 2008 and 2012. His campaign teams covered the whole ground to register voters and ask for their votes. Consequently, the 2008 and 2012 presidential polls registered two of the highest-ever voter turnouts in the history of the United States.[68]

The gift of diligence is, indeed, part of divine generosity to Barack Obama; and in the next section we will examine the signs of his diligence.

The Signs of Diligence

1. Certainly, his brilliant performances at Punahou School, Columbia University, and Harvard Law School could be attributed only to hard work, devotion, and care. These are the elements that cause his human intelligence to bear good fruits.

2. Surely, the spectacular coronation of his short political career with his election to the White House in 2008 was only the result of proper choice, careful timing, and commitment to work.

3. Moreover, during the campaign leading to the November 4, 2008, presidential election, Barack Obama and his team demonstrated a very high sense of diligence in organization, communication, and publicity. In fact, all the latest means of communication were put to use—radio, television, Internet, telephone, billboards, and newspapers.

4. Above all, the Obama teams made every effort to check and control the whole ballot, for regularity, fairness, and efficiency. And no less did they persuade qualified citizens to register and vote for Barack Obama. Consequently, the November 4, 2008, presidential polls registered a voter turnout of 64 percent,[68] with

over five million more voters participating than in 2004.

In the next section we will examine the sources from which Barack Obama derives his power of diligence.

The Sources of Diligence

The diligence of Barack Obama is derived from both spiritual and material sources. The spiritual origin of his diligence is his identity with the numbers three and four.

1. First, the number three, symbolizing perfect creation, action, and reaction, enables Barack Obama to act correctly and effectively to obtain the desired results.

2. Second, the power of the number three in Barack Obama is reinforced by that of the number four, which symbolizes firmness, strength, and regularity. The number four gives him the spirit of determination, hard work, vigilance, and prudence.

3. Finally, the material sources of the diligence of Barack Obama are his education and training. He attended the best schools in the United States—Punahou, Columbia, and Harvard. At these institutions diligence and excellence were essential requirements and not matters of choice. Definitely, that culture of commitment to work and the constant search for excellence awakened and strengthened his spiritual gift of diligence.

In the next section we will discover how the diligence of Barack Obama led to his victories in the November 4, 2008, and November 6, 2012, presidential elections. We will also discuss the ways he uses this weapon of diligence to win the tough battles of the White House.

The Power of Diligence

1. First, the diligence of Barack Obama enabled him to carry out more elaborate and effective presidential campaigns than his Republican challengers—Senator John McCain in 2008 and Governor Mitt Romney in 2012. And, as we mentioned above, his massive media campaigns and groundwork not only raised voter participation rates to record levels, but also earned him victory.

2. Second, the diligence of Barack Obama enabled him to get most of his supporters to register and vote for him. Otherwise, many of them would have been unable to vote—due to ignorance, apathy, or injustice at some voting stations.

3. Third, the exercise of diligence by Barack Obama and his volunteers enabled them to avoid costly mistakes and prevent fraud and other irregularities during the ballots. Of course, the American electoral system is the model of democracy and transparency in the world, but no human organization is completely free of bias and error. With everything so organized and monitored, the anticipated victory of Barack Obama in 2008 was therefore realized. And in 2012 the diligence of Barack Obama secured another victory for him, even when it was not anticipated.

4. Fourth, the virtue of diligence is an essential tool in the office of Barack Obama. It is with this weapon that he breaks the many hard nuts that trouble

the United States and the world today. Such issues include the financial crunch, unemployment, gay rights, terrorism, gun abuse, and climate change. The constant threat to the security of American citizens working or traveling abroad is another hot potato. Therefore, the weapon of diligence enables President Barack Obama to skillfully counter the threats of terrorism, war, nuclear arms, and piracy. In fact, he is now militarily engaged in the fight against terrorism, especially in Afghanistan and Pakistan. Also, his diplomatic engagements with the leaders of China, Russia, and Europe are aimed at preventing Iran and North Korea from building nuclear arsenals. In his second inaugural speech on January 21, 2013, he announced that "a decade of war is ending," and that "economic recovery has begun."[69]

5. Combined with his intelligence and courage, therefore, the diligence of Barack Obama is yielding very commendable results, and it is making change a real blessing for both the United States and the rest of the world. Definitely, the diligence of Barack Obama was a formidable and effective weapon in the 2012 presidential campaign. And it won for him a second mandate in the White House.

In chapter 17, we will look at the plague of darkness as a sacred weapon of Barack Obama.

---

68. US Census Bureau Reports, July 20, 2009.
69. CNN News, BBC News, January 21, 2013.

Artwork 18 of 21: Black Sphere.
This is the symbol of darkness.

CHAPTER SEVENTEEN

The Plague of Darkness

Moses raised his hand towards the sky, and there was total darkness throughout Egypt for three days. The Egyptians could not see each other, and no one left his house during that time. But the Israelites had light where they were living.

(Exodus 10:22–23)

THE previous chapter was about the plague of locusts as symbolizing the diligence of Barack Obama. In this chapter we will discuss the plague of darkness, which stands for the serenity of Barack Obama.

Background

Serenity is a powerful shield against calumny, intimidation, violence, and all kinds of adversity. It sustains inner peace and harmony; and thus it enhances mental, emotional, and physical balance. Serenity, therefore, upholds strength and confidence—which in turn improve one's performance.

The Plague of Darkness

In Exodus 10:21–23, the scriptures say, "The Lord then said to Moses, 'Raise your hand towards the sky, and darkness thick enough to be felt will cover the land of Egypt.' Moses raised his hand towards the sky, and there was total darkness throughout Egypt for three days. The Egyptians could not see each other, and no one left his house during that time. But the Israelites had light where they were living." Thus, like the plague of darkness, the serenity of Barack Obama covers all his opponents and detractors. It covers the merits of his competitors and hides him from those who try to assassinate him.

Serenity is one of the greatest weapons that Barack Obama has; he uses it often both to control himself and to subdue his adversaries. In the next section we will examine the evidence of serenity in Barack Obama.

The Signs of Serenity

1.   First, during the campaigns leading to the November 4, 2008, presidential election, Barack Obama challenged with icy calm all the attacks and accusations made against him by his opponents and detractors. He vigorously fought against the criticism of his lack of political experience, and he dismissed all allegations that he was a friend of Islam and connected to the militants who perpetrated the September 11, 2001, attacks on the United States. Yet, in his reactions

Barack Obama portrayed neither panic nor anger. And above all he did not seek revenge on his accusers.

2. Second, despite the confirmed assassination attempts made on Barack Obama[70] during the 2008 presidential campaign, he was not intimidated in any way. Instead, he pursued his campaign with audacious calm, courage, and confidence.

3. Finally, when the financial and economic situation in the United States got worse in 2008, Barack Obama was not frightened by the immensity of the task that he was going to face if elected president. On the contrary, he assured the public that change was still possible, although, given the financial crisis, it would require more time than expected for it to take form. And so he maintained his magic slogan, "Change, We Need," and they answered, "Yes, We Can."

In the next section we shall look for the sources from which Barack Obama receives his power of serenity.

The Sources of Serenity

The profound serenity of Barack Obama originates from both spiritual and human sources. From the spiritual plane, the serenity of Barack Obama derives from his identities with the numbers one, four, and eight.

1. The number one, representing God the Almighty, gives Barack Obama supremacy and dominion over his opponents. It also gives him mastership and control in difficult and challenging circumstances.

2. The number four, representing firmness, strength, and stability, gives Barack Obama the essential strength to face difficulty and adversity.

3. The number eight, representing double stability, sustains and strengthens his mental and emotional balance. This makes him calm, steady, and strong in all challenging and upsetting situations.

From the human plane, the sources of Barack Obama's serenity are his legal profession and his family background.

1. First, the exercise of the legal profession is characterized by a lot of debate, argumentation, adversity, and intimidation. Legal practice has, therefore, enabled Barack Obama to build a formidable shield of serenity all around his personality.

2. Second, the humble background of Barack Obama did not allow him to grow up with an inflated ego, which could easily be hurt by the vicious words and actions of other people.

3. Third, his familiarity with and sympathy for the less advantaged segments of society make him rather indifferent to stigmatization, insult, and calumny.

Obviously, the power of serenity played a key role in the victories of Barack Obama in the 2008 and 2012 presidential elections. In the next section we will look at how Barack Obama uses the weapon of serenity to conquer and exercise power.

The Power of Serenity

1. First, the serenity of Barack Obama boosted and sustained his mental and emotional equilibrium—especially during the three crucial debates with his archrivals John McCain in 2008[71] and Mitt Romney in 2012.

2. Second, the profound serenity of Barack Obama in 2008 in the backdrop of all the attacks on him was rather surprising. This serenity boosted his charm and popularity, given the fact that his opponent, John McCain, was most of the time embarrassed, nervous, and angry.

3. Third, the serenity of Barack Obama in 2008 proved that the man was not only prepared to face the challenges ahead of him, but also fit to be the master of the most powerful country on earth. Therefore, the serenity of Barack Obama is an essential tool for him to perform the enormous tasks that await him in the White House. With serenity, therefore, he is able to overcome everything that resists change, in order to make change a reality.

4. Fourth, his power of serenity continues to have a remarkable impact on the presidency of Barack Obama. It enables him to work with steadiness, confidence, and efficiency. He is also able to work with his opponents, both at home and abroad, with neither fear nor confrontation. Definitely, the serenity of Barack Obama enhances his strength and freedom to decide and to act. However, serenity requires a good mix of sympathy and receptivity so that it does not turn to callousness, indifference, and negligence. And,

evidently, Barack Obama is also well gifted with these two qualities.

5. Finally, the serenity of Barack Obama enabled him to stabilize and compose himself during the 2012 presidential campaign. And again he won the battle for the White House.

In chapter 18, we will look at the plague of the death of the firstborn as a sacred weapon of Barack Obama.

---

70. ABC News, October 27, 2008.
71. CNN Television (Barack Obama's first debate with John McCain), September 27, 2008.

Artwork 19 of 21: Human Head and Cross. This is the symbol of the dead firstborn.

CHAPTER EIGHTEEN

The Death of the Firstborn

> Then the Lord said to Moses, "I will send only one more punishment on the king of Egypt and his people. After that he will let you leave. In fact, he will drive all of you out of here." At midnight the Lord killed all the firstborn sons in Egypt, from the king's son who was heir to the throne to the son of the prisoner in the dungeon; all the firstborn of the animals were also killed. That night, the king, his officials, and all the other Egyptians were awakened. There was loud crying throughout Egypt, because there was not one home in which there was not a dead son.
>
> (Exodus 11:1; 12:29–30)

THE previous chapter was about the plague of darkness as symbolizing the serenity of Barack Obama. In this chapter we will look at the plague of the death of the firstborn, which represents the hope of Barack Obama.

Background

Hope is the most valuable thing that someone can lose. In fact, it is better to lose hold of all other things than to lose hold of hope. The matter of hope underlies both the essence of life and the reason for being. Thus the scripture says in Romans 8:24–25, "For it was by hope that we were saved; but if we see what we hope for, then it is not really hope. For which of us hopes for something we see? But if we hope for what we do not see, we wait for it with patience." However, hope without effort is as vain as effort without purpose. It is only when hope is linked to determination and purpose that life becomes active and productive. And it is so, despite its ups and downs, and pains and pleasures.

The Plague of the Death of the Firstborn

In Exodus 11:1; 12:29–31, it is written,

> Then the Lord said to Moses, "I will send only one more punishment on the king of Egypt and his people. After that he will let you leave. In fact, he will drive all of you out of here." At midnight the Lord killed all the firstborn sons in Egypt, from the king's son who was heir to the throne to the son of the prisoner in the dungeon; all the firstborn of the animals were also killed. That night, the king, his officials, and all the other Egyptians were awakened. There was loud crying throughout Egypt, because there was not one home in which there was not a dead son. That same night the king sent for Moses and Aaron and said, "Get out, you and your Israelites! Leave my country; go and worship the Lord, as you asked."

And like the plague of the death of the firstborn, the invincible hope of Barack Obama conquered all his challenges, and his victory killed the aspirations of his competitors. Thus there was loud crying throughout America, and beyond—cries of joy from his supporters, cries of sorrow from his detractors, and cries of wonderment from the skeptics.

Furthermore, in Exodus 12:40–42, the scripture says, "The Israelites had lived in Egypt for 430 years. On the day the 430 years ended, all the tribes of the Lord's people left Egypt. It was a night when the Lord kept watch to bring them out of Egypt; this same night is dedicated to the Lord for all time to come as a night when the Israelites must keep watch." Correspondingly, the United States became independent on July 4, 1776, and Barack Obama was first elected president of the United States on November 4, 2008. Between 1776 and 2008 there were 232 years, and between the time the Israelites were made slaves in Egypt and the time they left Egypt there were 430 years. The numerical reduction of 430 is equal to seven, and the numerical reduction of 232 is also equal to seven. Thus when we calculate $430 = 4 + 3 + 0 = 7$, we obtain seven; and also, when we calculate $232 = 2 + 3 + 2 = 7$, we obtain seven. So, as God commanded Moses and Aaron to free the Israelites from the burden of slavery, he also empowered Barack and Michelle Obama to free America from the spirit of racism. Thus America and the whole world kept watch on the night of November 4, 2008, to witness and celebrate the historic election of Barack Obama. And that date will forever be remembered as the day America was totally liberated from the yoke of racism, with the election of the first-ever African American president of the United States.

Finally, in Exodus 12:35–36, it is written, "The Israelites had done as Moses had said, and had asked the Egyptians for gold and silver jewelry and for clothing. The Lord made the Egyptians respect the people and give them what they asked for. In this way the Israelites carried away the wealth of the Egyptians." Thus the financial crunch that hit the United

States in 2008 and Hurricane Sandy,[72] which struck in 2012, only gave Barack Obama golden opportunities to demonstrate his solicitude and, hence, swing the electorate to his side. And from the rubble of the crunch and the hurricanes America emerges as a more united, powerful, and prosperous nation.

The power of hope of Barack Obama is so strong that it has made him a synonym of hope. In the next section we will examine the evidence of this hope.

The Signs of Hope

1. First, it was his hope in change that raised Barack Obama from humble birth, through diligence and determination, to statesmanship. He knew that to live was to hope, and that besides God, change is the only permanent reality.

2. Second, the hope of Barack Obama is evident in his speeches. For example, when he says, "America is a place where everything remains possible,"[73] it is a demonstration of his hope in the varied and unlimited abilities of the American people. And, no doubt, he also hopes to harness these abilities to rekindle the dream of the United States of America.

3. Third, Barack Obama kindles the hope to build a new world order, founded on peace and security. Practically, he turns the United States away from diplomatic dictatorship to interactive and constructive engagement. Under Barack Obama, therefore, America establishes her might and supremacy not on the premise of intimidation and force, but on that of freedom and justice.

4. Finally, the fact that, as an outsider, Barack Obama stood as candidate for the presidency of the United States in 2008 was a remarkable and convincing evidence of his power of hope. His hope was even so high that he could overcome the fact that no African American had done so before.

In the next section we will find out about the sources from which Barack Obama receives his power of hope.

The Sources of Hope

The spiritual origin of the hope of Barack Obama is his double identity with the numbers one and four.

1. First, the number one, as representative of God, gives Barack Obama unlimited possibilities. Thus in Luke 1:37, the scripture says, "For there is nothing that God cannot do." Therefore, the number one, which is the source of everything, is also the source of hope.

2. Second, the number four gives Barack Obama the power of endurance and firmness, which sustain his determination to realize what he hopes for.

However, the hope of Barack Obama was also developed from human sources.

1. First, his unstable family condition when he was an infant not only initiated him into the world of change, but also germinated his inherent seed of hope, which was later to be nurtured by his courage.

2. Finally, the fact that his childhood in Jakarta and studentship in New York City brought him into

contact with rather revolting human conditions also fueled his hope for change. Therefore, the hope of Barack Obama is intimately associated with sympathy and audacity. And these constantly drive his determination to bring change where and when it is necessary.

In the next section we will discuss how Barack Obama uses the weapon of hope to win and exercise power in the White House.

The Power of Hope

1. First, the hope of Barack Obama, as demonstrated in his candidacy for the presidency, gave him the opportunity to exhibit his previously unknown qualities. These, in fact, outweighed his weaknesses—especially those of the racial prejudice of others and the want of long political experience. This exposure, then, earned him admiration, trust, and victory. This demonstrates what has earlier been called the law of the triangle—that when the hope for change met with the necessity for change in 2008, the first election of Barack Obama became inevitable.

2. Second, Barack Obama's hope for the presidency of the United States was not an end in itself. Rather, it was a stepping-stone to his hope for change. Thus when he declares that "the ways of Washington must change," he hopes to make the American dream real to all Americans. Therefore, he is actively working to consolidate the diversity and openness of the United States, in order to enhance her progress and supremacy. This is evident from his January 29, 2013, initiative to

legalize about eleven million illegal immigrants in the United States while tightening the seal on the borders.

3. Third, the power of hope of Barack Obama continues to inflame his determination, courage, and ingenuity for the concretization of his dreams and campaign promises. Evidently, Barack Obama does not want to betray the profound trust the entire world now bestows on him as the hope of the twenty-first century.

4. Fourth, Barack Obama has proved that he can do extraordinary things, that he can pass where others have stuck, and that he can succeed where many have failed. And, having lived the first miracle of hope, his historic election to the White House in 2008, nothing else could stop him from hoping for another victory in 2012. Thus with the weapon of hope, on November 6, 2012, Barack Obama became the seventeenth personality and first African American to be elected and reelected as president of the United States of America.

5. Finally, by transforming himself from nothing to something, Barack Obama was taking a fundamental step to transform America and the whole world. And this is the hope that he brought—the hope for change. So the spirit of hope gripped the world as an infectious virus, and since the historic election of Barack Obama in 2008, there is nothing more that humanity cannot do.

In chapter 19, we will discuss the change to Barack Obama and his impact on change.

---

72. CNN News, October 29, 2009.

73. Barack Obama, *Our Enduring Spirit: President Barack Obama's First Words to America* (New York: HarperCollins, 2009).

Artwork 20 of 21: Turning Wheel. This is the symbol of movement, transformation, and change.

CHAPTER NINETEEN

The Wheel of Change

> Jesus is the one of whom the scripture says,
> "The stone that you the builders despised
> turned out to be the most important of all."
> Salvation is to be found through him alone;
> in all the world there is no one else whom God
> has given who can save us.
>
> (Acts 4:11–12)

IN the last chapter we discussed the plague of the death of the firstborn as symbolizing Barack Obama's holy weapon of hope. We will now discuss change as a synonym for Barack Obama, as well as the impact he has made on change.

Background

Of all realities that are known to exist, only two are permanent—God and change. "Change alone is unchanging;" said Heraclitus of Ephesus (535BCE-475BCE), "no man ever steps in the same river twice, for it's not the same river and he's not the same man." Those who resist change are enemies of God, and those who ignore God are victims of change. Therefore, like God, change is something that was, is, and always will be. Thus society, people, life, and nature are always on the move. Nothing is always the same; everything changes. Change is contagious because everything is related to everything else, as all things are related to God. A change in one thing, therefore, causes other things to change, either to accommodate the change or to oppose it.

Furthermore, change is both spontaneous and inevitable—it takes place anywhere, at any time, and by any means. Change has a will and a purpose, which only God knows and commands. And in the absolute, change is indifferent to the wishes of anyone in particular. Therefore, one can change only what is changeable, and maintain only what is unchangeable.

The Importance of Change

Every change has a purpose, which is always good, notwithstanding that the immediate outcome may be painful. God alone holds the key to the mystery of change, but what is obvious is that every change is intended to bring a benefit, either in the instant or in the future. In life, change comes to remove monotony, boredom, weakness, and above all, the evils of continuity. For everything that is not God is always changing to perfection, either willingly or unwillingly. So in Romans 8:28–30, the scripture says, "We know that in all things God works for good with those who love him, those he has called according to his purpose. Those whom God had already chosen he also set apart to become like his Son, so that the Son would be the eldest brother in a large family. And so those whom God set apart, he called; and those he called, he put right with himself, and he shared his glory with them."

The Change to Barack Obama

The will of change to Barack Obama is, therefore, in the power of God, but on the objective plane we can identify five main factors that caused this amazing change.

1. First, the fundamental ideology and political program of Barack Obama in 2008 was in favor of the underprivileged. And, especially, it was a time of deepening social and economic misery, which was affecting the United States of America. In fact, his social plan was concretely backed by his past actions in favor of the poor South Side residents in Chicago.

2. Second, the mixed origin and color of Barack Obama is really symbolic of the multiracial society of the United States, which is constantly searching for equilibrium on the fulcrum of equality and social justice.

3. Third, the impressive qualities of Barack Obama— notably his courage, charm, oratory, and serenity— are very powerful and effective weapons. In fact, they paved his way from the primaries, through his nomination as the Democratic Party presidential candidate, to his election as the forty-fourth president of the United States.

4. Fourth, in 2008 the unpopularity of George Walker Bush and the Republican Party, both at home and abroad, was outstanding. That was the outcome of eight years of diplomatic dictatorship and military spending. Moreover, the external hostility of the Bush administration led to increasing threats to the security of the United States from Islamic militants. In those

circumstances, there was a strong tendency for the electorate to sanction the Republican Party in favor of the Democratic Party, no matter who their candidates were. The preference, therefore, was for anyone who would broker peace and ensure real security for America and her citizens. And, upon the assessment of the main contenders, the stature of Barack Obama was the most convincing.

5.   However, the final incident that strengthened the position of Barack Obama was the very unprecedented financial crunch that hit the United States of America, and spread to the rest of the world, in the heat of the 2008 campaign for the White House. The hard financial crunch not only threatened to reverse the American dream, it was already causing massive unemployment and social misery throughout the United States. It was, therefore, imperative to find a messiah, and in the circumstances, there was no other name than that of Barack Obama. This corresponds with what the scripture says in Acts 4:11–12: "Jesus is the one of whom the scripture says, 'The stone that you the builders despised turned out to be the most important of all.' Salvation is to be found through him alone; in all the world there is no one else whom God has given who can save us."

Definitely, Barack Obama is not Jesus Christ, but he is a sample of the number two—the messiah—who was initially despised because of his color and inexperience. Then his social and economic program brought hope. And, moreover, he had previously distinguished himself as a dedicated social worker when he worked to help poor Chicago South Side residents cope with a wave of plant closings. Therefore, the change to Barack Obama was made from heaven. For, notwithstanding that he started off as an outsider, changing circumstances later played in his favor and ushered him into the White House.

We have earlier stated that change always leads to change. Certainly, the change to Barack Obama was not made for its own sake but for the sake of change that he would make. In the next section we will discuss the impact that Barack Obama makes on change.

The Change by Barack Obama

1. First, the most urgent change that Barack Obama brought to overturn the financial crisis and revive the economy of the United States was his February 17, 2009, economic stimulus budget of $787 billion. That was very necessary to save existing jobs and to create new ones. Thus, facing the unprecedented economic downturn at the beginning of his first mandate, Barack Obama successfully pushed the Congress to vote trillions of dollars to bail out strategic corporations, such as General Motors, in order to secure jobs and relaunch the economy.

   Logically, the poor performance of the economy during the first administration of Barack Obama was a result of the financial crunch that he inherited. However, by the end of his first mandate he had already stabilized the financial markets and was looking forward to relaunched economic growth. Thus, on January 7, 2011, *Think Progress* reported, "Responding to the jobs report, House Minority Leader Nancy Pelosi (D-CA) noted that President Obama and the Democratic Congress have created 'more jobs in 2010 than President Bush did over eight years.'" Indeed, from February 2001, Bush's first full month in office, through January 2009—his last—the economy added just 1 million jobs. By contrast, in 2010 alone, the economy added at least 1.1 million jobs. As the *Wall Street Journal* noted, in the last month of Bush's term the former president had the "worst track record for job creation since the government began keeping records. And job creation under Bush was anemic long before the recession began." And, on March 23, 2012, the *New York Times* wrote,

> As the presidential election campaign heats up, two measures of the economic success of President Obama's administration provide drastically different views of how he has done. His stock market record is among the best of all the administrations that have held office over the last century. But in terms of economic growth, the record is among the poorest. But since the presidential inauguration on Jan. 20, 2009, the stock market has risen at an annual rate of 16.4 percent, even after adjusting for inflation.

2. Second, Barack Obama took very conspicuous steps to protect housing and to guarantee health care and Social Security for all. On March 22, 2010, he successfully pressed Congress to pass his debated health-care bill, thus allowing millions of Americans access to comprehensive health care. On January 21, 2013, Barack Obama restated that universal health care was one of the priorities of his second term in the White House.[74]

3. Third, Barack Obama became actively engaged in constructive diplomacy, as opposed to the arrogance and dictatorship of his predecessor, George W. Bush. In fact, it was time for the United States to make friends with her enemies and to take a more compromising and concerted approach to international and bilateral

issues. That was the Obama way to polish the face of the United States and to suppress terrorist activity around the world. This constructive engagement inevitably leads to world peace and stability, while holding the balance of power in favor of the United States.

4. Fourth, under Barack Obama the United States has intervened not only where her interests are at stake, but wherever necessary, to prevent or settle conflicts. Although Israel and the Palestinian Authority are still at daggers drawn, the diplomacy of Barack Obama has significantly reduced tension in the Middle East, and it will eventually lead to the final settlement of the Palestinians' question of an independent territory. In 2011 he called back the remaining contingent of American troops from Iraq and ended the American occupation of that country. He is currently engaged, politically and militarily, against Islamic insurgents in Afghanistan and Pakistan. And in Syria the Obama administration is aiding the rebels to overthrow the dictatorial regime in Damascus.

5. Fifth, under the direction of President Barack Obama, American special forces tracked down and killed the leader of Al Qaeda, Osama bin Laden, on May 2, 2011.[75] That was a remarkable achievement, given that Al Qaeda remains the greatest enemy of the United States. And the predecessor of Barack Obama, George W. Bush, had hunted Osama bin Laden for seven years in vain.

6. Finally, the crowning achievement of Barack Obama was his reelection on November 6, 2012, to a second term of office as president of the United States. Thus he became the first African American to be elected

and reelected to the White House, and the seventeenth American president to win two mandates.

However, despite the brilliant successes of Barack Obama so far, many challenges still face him at home and abroad. He needed a second mandate in order to overcome these challenges and to fully realize his dreams—and he got it. In the next section we will touch on some of these stubborn stones.

The Stubborn Stones

1. First, Barack Obama is still struggling to control the frequent and fatal abuse of guns in the United States. The right to carry guns is increasingly becoming a matter of controversy. There have been many public protests in the United States against this right, and although the conservatives still hold very strongly to it, there is now good reason and growing concern for the law to change. In fact, the guns that were intended to be used by the righteous against the wicked are now being used by the wicked against the righteous. Of course, it is logical to think that when everyone is armed, the guns protect no one but the offenders, because they are the first to shoot. The twenty-three executive orders signed by President Barack Obama on January 16, 2013, to control gun sales and ban "weapons of war" and "assault weapons" are some of the bold steps he is taking to fight the abuse of guns in the United States.[76] Unfortunately, the National Rifle Association continues to fight to block any legislation intended to control gun rights.

2. Second, unemployment is still a serious problem in the United States—about 14.5 million Americans are still without jobs. Moreover, the staggering $16 trillion

US public debt is one of the hardest American nuts to crack. And Barack Obama is expected to overcome these challenges before he leaves office in January 2017.

3. Third, although the United States ratified the 1992 Kyoto convention on climate change, she has to take more concrete action in reducing her carbon emissions into the atmosphere. In fact, America must lead the world in developing clean alternative and renewable energy. No doubt, the fight against climate change and the development of sustainable energy were two key points in the second inaugural speech of President Barack Obama on January 21, 2013.

4. Fourth, despite the elimination of Osama bin Laden, terrorism remains the greatest threat to security in America and the whole world. In addition, piracy often threatens peace in the Horn of Africa, the Indian Ocean, the Gulf of Guinea, and many other places. And Islamic militants are trying to gain substantial grounds in the Sahara, northern Nigeria, and the Middle East. Surely, Barack Obama and the United States will not remain indifferent to these inhumane activities.

5. Finally, with Iran and North Korea stubbornly developing nuclear weapons, the threat of a nuclear holocaust still looms upon the world. This is a major challenge to Barack Obama, as president of the United States. And, of course, he is not taking the threat lying down. In fact, he is actively persuading Russia and China to press on their allies, Iran and North Korea, to denounce their nuclear ambitions. Ultimately, these concerted and constructive engagements will bear fruits, and nuclear war will be won peacefully.

Now, it is irrelevant whether or not change by Barack Obama is what everybody wants. The important thing to know is that, as it is written in Ecclesiastes 3:1, 11–13, "Everything that happens in this world happens at the time that God chooses. He has set the right time for everything. He has given us a desire to know the future, but never gives us the satisfaction of fully understanding what he does. So I realized that all we can do is to be happy and do the best we can while we are still alive."

In the epilogue, we will discuss the significance of the election and reelection of Barack Obama as the first African American president of the United States.

---

74. BBC News, January 21, 2013.

75. BBC News, May 2, 2011.

76. BBC News, January 16, 2013.

Artwork 21 of 21: Orb. This is the symbol of majesty, power, and supremacy.

The Supremacy of God

"My thoughts," says the Lord, "are not like yours, and my ways are different from yours. As high as the heavens are above the earth, so high are my ways and thoughts above yours."

(Isaiah 55:8–9)

THE last chapter examined the causes of change to Barack Obama and the impact of Barack Obama on change. In the epilogue we will discuss the significance of the election and reelection of Barack Obama as the first-ever African American president of the United States.

Those events testified to the might and supremacy of God. He alone is the Creator and ruler of the universe. He is the keeper of time and the master of space; he shares his glory with no other god. Thus the scripture says, in Isaiah 43:10–13,

> People of Israel, you are my witnesses; I chose you
> to be my servant, so that you would know me and

believe in me and understand that I am the only God. Besides me there is no other god; there never was and never will be. I alone am the Lord, the only one who can save you. I predicted what would happen, and then I came to your aid. No foreign god has ever done this; you are my witnesses. I am God and always will be. No one can escape from my power; no one can change what I do.

God Rewards Good

1. The first significance of these events is that every good work earns its reward at the right time. When Barack Obama was helping poor Chicago South Side residents to cope with a wave of plant closings in the 1980s, he did not know that in 2008 he would be called to the same mission at the federal level—to save America from an unprecedented financial crisis, mass plant closings, and widespread unemployment. Thus God rewarded him and gave him the privilege to serve as president of the most powerful country in the world.

2. The second significance is that merit is still being recognized, despite the corruption and imperfections of human society. Therefore, from a human perspective, the great virtues of Barack Obama, which have been discussed in this book, justify God's favor on him to be elected and reelected president of the United States. For in John 15:1–2, 7–8, the scriptures say,

> I [Jesus] am the real vine, and my Father is the gardener. He breaks off every branch in me that does not bear fruit, and he prunes every branch that does bear fruit, so that it will be clean and bear more fruit.

> If you remain in me and my words remain in you, then you will ask for anything you wish, and you shall have it. My Father's glory is shown by your bearing much fruit; and in this way you become my disciples.

3. The third significance of the election and reelection of Barack Obama to the White House is that all people and races are equal before God, and that stigmatization and prejudice come only from the egos of human beings. Furthermore, it proves that the United States is fully matured, for racial equality has progressed from a constitutional provision to a social reality. This corresponds with scriptures in Galatians 3:26–29:

> It is through faith that all of you are God's children in union with Christ Jesus. You were baptized into union with Christ, and now you are clothed, so to speak, with the life of Christ himself. So there is no difference between Jews and Gentiles, between slaves and free people, between men and women; you are all one in union with Christ Jesus. If you belong to Christ, then you are the descendants of Abraham and will receive what God has promised.

Hope in God

4. The fourth significance of the election and reelection of Barack Obama as president of the United States is that it confirms the old saying: no condition is permanent. In fact, everything is constantly changing, within the plan and according to the will of God. Therefore, hope is the greatest thing that we have, and it is also the only thing that we must not lose. The victories of Barack Obama prove that hope is an invisible lane that leads

anyone who hopes to where he or she wants. And hope does not fail when it is put on God the Almighty. Thus, the scripture says in Romans 8:24–25, "For it was by hope that we were saved; but if we see what we hope for, then it is not really hope. For which of us hopes for something we see? But if we hope for what we do not see, we wait for it with patience."

5.   The fifth significance of the election of Barack Obama is that the realization of what we hope for occurs always at the most proper time. And this is to serve the will of God and to satisfy the necessity for change. Therefore, God's time is always the best. And so, from Martin Luther King Jr. to Barack Hussein Obama Jr., and from black slaves to black masters, centuries passed and blood poured out, for God's time had not yet come. Thus in John 2:3–5, 7–11, the scriptures say,

> When the wine had given out, Jesus' mother said to him, "They have no wine left." "You must not tell me what to do," Jesus replied. "My time has not yet come." Jesus' mother then told the servants, "Do whatever he tells you." Jesus said to the servants, "Fill these jars with water." They filled them to the brim, and then he told them, "Now draw some water out and take it to the man in charge of the feast." They took him the water, which now had turned into wine, and he tasted it. He did not know where this wine had come from (but, of course, the servants who had drawn out the water knew); so he called the bridegroom and said to him, "Everyone else serves the best wine first, and after the guests have had plenty to drink, he serves the ordinary wine. But you have kept the best wine until now!" Jesus performed this first miracle in Cana in Galilee; there he revealed his glory, and his disciples believed in him.

The Mystery of God

6. The sixth significance of the victories of Barack Obama is that the ways of God are mysterious—no one can tell how God will act to fulfill his plan or to answer the prayers of his people. Thus in Isaiah 55:8–9, the scriptures say, "'My thoughts', says the Lord, 'are not like yours, and my ways are different from yours. As high as the heavens are above the earth, so high are my ways and thoughts above yours.'" Accordingly, we noted that many of the events that favored the election of Barack Obama happened unexpectedly and just at the right time to influence the voters.

    The first of these events was the financial crunch in 2008, which shifted the presidential debate from foreign policy to the economy. And there, Barack Obama had a comparative advantage over his challenger, John McCain. The second phenomenon in 2008 was the record unpopularity of the outgoing Republican president, George Walker Bush. It affected the Republican presidential candidate, Senator John McCain, giving him a severe disadvantage. The third factor in 2008 was the huge human, financial, and material losses to America resulting from her military occupation of Iraq. There were, therefore, increasingly persistent calls from compatriots for American soldiers to return home. This favored the candidacy of Barack Obama because he was fundamentally opposed to the American invasion of Iraq, and he had a plan: the immediate withdrawal of American forces from Iraq if he was elected president.

    Finally, the significant increase in the previous years of the nonwhite population of the United States, through immigration and higher birth rates among them, worked to the advantage of Barack Obama. In fact, this segment of the American population, which used to be reluctant to vote, actually voted in 2008 because they were excited about the candidacy of Barack Obama. Moreover, they were actively and effectively encouraged by Barack Obama's teams of volunteers, who assisted them to register and to vote. The result was that the 2008 US presidential election had a record voter turnout of over 64 percent; and almost all new or first-time voters voted for Barack Obama.

7. The seventh significance of the election and reelection of Barack Obama as the first African American president of the United States is that God is all-powerful. Certainly, none of the events mentioned above were initiated or arranged for by Barack Obama. And no one ever saw them coming to support his candidacy; God put them in place to show his mighty power. Thus the scriptures say in Mark 10:27, "Jesus looked straight at them and answered, 'This is impossible for human beings, but not for God; everything is possible for God.'" And in Luke 1:37, it is written, "For there is nothing that God cannot do."

The Will of God

In fact, God wills anything and does it—as he wants, where he wants, when he wants, and how he wants. Therefore, no one can claim merit for anything done or undone. And no matter one's ability or power, one can do only what God approves. Thus, in 2 Corinthians 10:17–18, it is written, "But as the scripture says, 'Whoever wants to boast must boast about what the Lord has done.' For it is people of whom the Lord thinks well who are really approved, not people who think well of themselves." But we are comfortable in the fact that God's plan for us is always perfect and good. In Jeremiah 29:10–11, it is also written, "The Lord says, 'When Babylon's seventy years are over, I will show my concern for you and keep my promise to bring you back home. I alone know the plans I have for you; plans to bring you prosperity and not disaster, plans to bring about the future you hope for.'" And so, from the American Declaration of Independence in 1776 to the first election of Barack Obama in 2008, *seventy years* had passed: for the numerical difference between 2008 and 1776 is equal to 232; and the numerical reductions of 232 and 70 are both equal to seven. Thus, when we calculate 2 + 3 + 2 = 7, we obtain seven, and also when we calculate 7 + 0 = 7, we obtain seven. Therefore, the election and reelection of Barack Obama fulfill God's plan to bring freedom, prosperity, and hope to the "chosen" people of America.

And his ordination corresponds with what is written in Revelation 5:7–10:

> The Lamb went and took the scroll from the right hand of the one who sits on the throne. As he did so, the four living creatures and the twenty-four elders fell down before the Lamb. Each had a harp and gold bowls filled with incense, which are the prayers of God's people. They sang a new song: "You are worthy to take the scroll and to break open its seals. For you were killed, and by your sacrificial death you bought for God people from every tribe, language, nation, and race. You have made them a kingdom of priests to serve our God, and they shall rule on earth."

Therefore, as the scripture says in Revelation 4:11, we proclaim, "Our Lord and God! You are worthy to receive glory, honor, and power. For you created all things, and by your will they were given existence and life." Amen.

References

News & Information

CNN World

BBC World Service

ABC News

Online Resources

www.barackobama.com

www.barack-obama-bio.com

www.america.gov

Wikipedia

References

Casciaro, J. M., and J. M. Forte. *God, the World and Man in the Message of the Bible*. Dublin: Four Courts, 1996.

Decos, Hans. *Numerology: Key to Your Inner Self*. New York: Penguin Putnam, 1994.

Drayer, Ruth A. *Numerology: The Power in Numbers*. New York: Square One Publishers, 2003.

Hornby, A. S. *Oxford Advanced Learner's Dictionary of Current English*. Oxford: Oxford University Press, 2000.

Kennedy, Edward M. *The American Journey of Barack Obama*. New York: Little, Brown & Co., 2008.

Lowe, E. J. *A Survey of Metaphysics*. New York: Oxford University Press, 2002.

Lowe, William L. *Philosophy of Religion: An Introduction*. Los Angeles: Wadsworth, 2006.

Monforte, Josemaria. *Getting to Know the Bible*. Princeton: Scepter Publishers, 1998.

Montague, George. *Understanding the Bible: A Basic Introduction to Biblical Interpretation*. New York: Paulist Press, 1997.

O'Reilly, Bill, and Martin Dugard. *Killing Lincoln: The Shocking Assassination That Changed America Forever*. New York: Henry Holt & Co., 2011.

Obama, Barack. *Change We Can Believe In: Barack Obama's Plan to Renew America's Promise*. New York: Crown Publishing, 2008.

Obama, Barack. *Dreams from My Father*. New York: Crown Publishing, 2004.

Obama, Barack. *Our Enduring Spirit: President Barack Obama's First Words to America*. New York: HarperCollins, 2009.

Obama, Barack. *The Audacity of Hope*. New York: Crown Publishing, 2006.

Obama, Barack. *The Essential Barack Obama: The Grammy Award–Winning Recordings by Barack Obama*. New York: Random House, 2008.

Orchard, Dom Bernard. *Born to Be King: The Epic of the Incarnation*. London: Ealing Abbey, 1993.

Phillips, David A. *The Complete Book of Numerology*. Los Angeles: Hay House, 2005.

Taylor, Richard. *Metaphysics*. 4th ed. Boston: Pearson, 1991.

United Bible Societies. *Good News Bible*. New York: American Bible Society, 1994.

Wolffe, Richard. *Renegade: The Making of a President*. New York: Crown Publishing, 2009.

Wright, Nicolas T. *Jesus and the Victory of God*. Minneapolis: Fortress, 1996.

Wright, Nicolas T. *The New Testament and the People of God*. Minneapolis: Fortress, 1992.

ABOUT THE AUTHOR

AYING Godman is an eminent biblical scholar, Christian mystic, and numerologist. He is a teaching minister in the Catholic Charismatic Renewal Movement of the Roman Catholic Church in Cameroon. A keen student of metaphysics and current affairs, he has been studying Barack Obama's career since 2006.